SURVIVAL SKILLS FOR SCHOLARS

DEALING WITH ETHICAL DILEMMAS ON CAMPUS

MARCIA LYNN WHICKER
JENNIE JACOBS KRONENFELD

SAGE Publications
International Educational and Professional Publisher
Thousand Oaks   London   New Delhi

For information address:

 SAGE Publications, Inc.
2455 Teller Road
Thousand Oaks, California 91320

SAGE Publications Ltd.
6 Bonhill Street
London EC2A 4PU
United Kingdom

SAGE Publications India Pvt. Ltd.
M-32 Market
Greater Kailash I
New Delhi 110 048 India

Printed in the United States of America

Library of Congress Cataloging-in-Publication Data

Whicker, Marcia Lynn.
    Dealing with ethical dilemmas on campus / authors, Marcia Lynn Whicker, Jennie Jacobs Kronenfeld.
        p. cm.   — (Survival skills for scholars; v. 14)
    Includes bibliographical references.
    ISBN 0-8039-5480-8.   — ISBN 0-8039-5481-6 (pbk.)
    1. College teachers, Professional ethics.   I. Kronenfeld, Jennie Jacobs II. Title. III. Series.
LB1779.W55   1994
174'.9372—dc20   94-18899

94 95 96 97 98 10 9 8 7 6 5 4 3 2 1

DEALING WITH ETHICAL DILEMMAS ON CAMPUS

SURVIVAL SKILLS FOR SCHOLARS

Managing Editor: Mitchell Allen

Survival Skills for Scholars provides you, the professor or advanced graduate student working in a college or university setting, with practical
suggestions for making the most of your academic career. These brief,
readable guides will help you with skills that you are required to master as
a college professor but may have never been taught in graduate school.
Using hands-on, jargon-free advice and examples, forms, lists, and suggestions for additional resources, experts on different aspects of academic life give
invaluable tips on managing the day-to-day tasks of academia—effectively
and efficiently.

Volumes in This Series

Contents

PART I

When Ethics, Politics, and the Law Collide

1 | Why You Should Care About Ethical Dilemmas

In an ideal academic world of ivy-covered walls, all colleagues would be ethical, what is moral would be obvious, and ethical behavior would always prevail. However, although modern universities and colleges are often vibrant and challenging places to work, members of academia are pressured by the public, by legislators, by funding agencies, and by parents. Therefore, they are far from a tranquil ideal where the aggregated behavior of individual monastic scholars results in unambiguously ethical outcomes. This book is about colleagues who sometimes, or even often, are unethical. It is about episodes that people in universities and colleges prefer not to talk about except in whispers, if at all—clashes over ethics and the dilemmas created by unethical colleagues in research and teaching. Unfortunately, ethical dilemmas arise with an unknown but likely greater frequency than is commonly acknowledged, especially to outsiders. Indeed, most faculty and administrators wish that such potentially career-derailing episodes would go away, because the reality is that unethical colleagues create problems for those who work with them as well as for themselves. However, ignoring unethical colleagues and ethical dilemmas and pretending they do not exist does not make them go away.

3

The behavior of unethical colleagues causes moral anguish. It makes one uncomfortable and anxious. Accusing a colleague of wrongdoing is not easy or fun. Ethical dilemmas often become adversarial, pitting colleague against colleague and faculty against administrators. Feelings may run high, political mistakes may be made, perspectives may get muddied, and unmitigated reality may prove elusive. How you deal with ethical dilemmas may affect your career. Also, ethical dilemmas are not always clear-cut; often both sides in the struggle have mixed motives, including some selfish ones.

Perhaps in your career you have escaped, until now, the dilemma, the angst, and the pain of confronting an unethical colleague. Until you have to deal with an ethical dilemma, you may walk in the land of the idealists and the skeptics. Idealists believe that universities, by virtue of their special role in society as guardians of truth and generators of knowledge, are spared the unethical behavior and the moral dilemmas that arise in other institutions, including government and business. Instead of blaming the institutional processes that allowed the dilemmas to occur or the perpetrators of wrongdoing, skeptics tend to blame the innocent people who are inadvertently and unexpectedly trapped in such dilemmas as politically naive.

But those of you who have experienced or watched a close friend or colleague grapple with an ethical dilemma, walk among those who are aware of the grave implications of ethical dilemmas for all involved—the university or college in which wrongdoing transpires, those who engage in actions that created the dilemma, and even and especially those who discover and uncover the improper and immoral action. It is for this latter group—for you who are struggling with how to address wrongdoing you wish you had not seen but now cannot easily ignore—that this book is written.

Your reaction to an ethical dilemma may be affected by the power you hold within the university and the academic community, because the consequences of your response are in large part a function of the professional power you hold or can access as well as how right you are. That is what this book is about.

Lest you think you are immune from the impact of unethical behavior, consider the findings of a nationwide study conducted by Swazey, Louis, and Anderson (1994). These authors used data from a survey of 2,000 faculty members and 2,000 doctoral students in departments of chemistry, civil engineering, microbiology, and sociology at major research universities. They also conducted in-depth interviews in eight departments. Their conclusions are shocking.

First, they found that unethical behavior is significantly underreported. Both faculty and doctoral students knew of substantially more incidents of unethical behavior than they reported. Of faculty respondents, 22% said they knew of department members' overlooking sloppy use of data, and one third knew of cases of inappropriate credit being given or taken for research papers. Another 40% knew colleagues who inappropriately had used university resources for personal ends. Other forms of misbehavior were also underreported. These included ignoring policies on biosafety and on research with animal and human subjects; sexual harassment and discrimination; and cheating by graduate students.

Second, Swazey, Louis, and Anderson found that fear of retaliation for reporting wrongdoing was the key factor in underreporting. Over 50% of the graduate students surveyed felt they would experience retaliation for reporting faculty wrongdoing, and 29% feared retaliation for reporting fellow graduate students. Substantial proportions of faculty also expressed concern about retaliation for reporting ethical violations. Forty percent felt they would experience retaliation for reporting a graduate student, and 65% believed retaliation would result if they reported a colleague's unethical behavior.

Faculty were conflicted over their beliefs about what should be done to monitor ethical violations. Although 94% believed that academics should exercise collective responsibility for the conduct of their professional colleagues, only 13% believed that departments actually exercise such responsibility over fellow faculty members. Nor did faculty think that greater control was exercised over graduate students. Although nearly all (99%) believed that academics should exercise collective responsibility for the conduct of graduate students, only 27% believed such monitoring and control actually occurred.

The Difficulty of Setting Unambiguous Standards for Ethical Behavior in Universities

The problem of setting and abiding by ethical codes of conduct is not unique to universities and colleges. All complex organizations confront these tasks. How well these tasks are performed contributes to the overall productivity both of an organization and of specific employees. Where codes of ethics are widely recognized, fair, reasonable, and uniformly applied, productivity is enhanced. Where codes of ethics are poorly defined, lack consensus, are perceived as unreasonable, and are arbitrarily enforced, productivity may suffer.

Establishing and enforcing a reasonable code of ethics in academic environments may be particularly challenging for several reasons, which are described below.

Universities and colleges are complex organizations whose employees perform highly specialized work. Codes of ethics are more difficult to establish for complex organizations than for simple ones. In simple organizations, work is relatively homogenous and standardized. A uniform set of standards can be developed to apply to all employees. In complex organizations, however, work is not homogenous. Different standards of conduct are more likely to emerge that are appropriate for the function of the unit or department but are not as pertinent to other departments.

The difficulty of setting ethical codes in academic settings is complicated, too, by the complex character of the expected work. Research and scholarly publication have always been an important academic activity, especially in large universities.

However, today, most colleges as well as universities expect some research and publications. Monitoring these with ethical standards is difficult—from the appropriate conduct of research on human subjects in the biological and medical fields to questions of racism in the humanities and arts. Teaching is also a complex activity with many facets and few direct standards for measuring performance, other than often controversial student evaluations. Complexity in organizational structure and the character of the work performed, in turn, make the establishment of ethical codes not impossible, but more difficult.

Academic departments and schools often have great autonomy. In part, because of their complexity, academic departments, schools, and other subunits often have great autonomy in making decisions about work and faculty and student welfare. This autonomy contributes to variations across units in what is expected and accepted. Although variation may commonly occur on questions of productivity and performance, expectations about ethical behavior may also vary. Units, then, become as good as their leadership and the faculty within them.

Faculty may have tenure, which limits normal administrative discretion. Because of faculty tenure, the carrot-and-stick range that university and college administrators have to enforce codes of ethics is much more restricted than for a normal business setting. In particular, the threat of firing an unethical employee, always implicit in many nonacademic organizations, is largely missing in the academy for tenured faculty. Firing tenure faculty is perceived as such a blunt club that it is rarely wielded, even in cases of acknowledged wrongdoing. Nor are pay cuts used with any frequency to enforce ethical behavior. Instead, the range of sanctions for unethical behavior includes high teaching loads, cutting travel money, assigning unpopular class times, rigid adherence to rules that otherwise would not be rigidly enforced, and assignment of poor or limited office space.

Universities are peer regulated, resembling legislatures more than bureaucracies. In hierarchical bureaucracies, top officials can more easily issue directives regulating behavior than in bodies of peers, such as most legislatures. Given the shift toward participative management, even officials in bureaucracies cannot easily take action without some consultation with lower level employees. But the consultation and consensus development surrounding decision making in peer-regulated bodies is much greater. Universities are not unique in difficulties regulating unethical behavior that stem from the importance of decision-making by peers. Congress often finds monitoring unethical behavior by members troublesome, as the case of Senator Robert Packwood indicates. Only after considerable pressure from both victims of Packwood's sexual harassment and from the public did Congress begin to explore the charges against Packwood. In universities, the peer nature of decisions makes arriving at a consensus sometimes difficult, especially over controversial ethical issues. Under the best conditions, compromise and negotiation result in a reasonable outcome. Under less salutary conditions, indecisiveness and stalemate may result.

Standards of ethical conduct may vary somewhat across disciplines. Disciplinary norms as well as departmental norms may impact on what is judged appropriate and ethical behavior. Scientific disciplines, for example, tend to be more lax in determining who should receive credit for research activities, because large experiments and other scientific projects often involve many people, all of whom claim credit. Yet these disciplines are often more rigid in defining acceptable research methodologies and procedures. On the other hand, the humanities and arts tend to be more lax in defining appropriate approaches to a subject matter and are very strict about parceling out academic credit for authorship or for creation of a particular work.

The difficulty of setting unambiguous, fair, and nonarbitrary standards of ethical behavior in academic environments allows and even forces many judgment calls about what is ethical and what is not. It also allows the unethical behavior to go undetected, and, when discovered, sometimes unpunished. Consider the following events from the life of one academician.

A Not-So-Nice Story

Mike sat hunched over his desk, angry, sad, depressed, and exhausted. The faculty in his department at Midstate University (MU) were badly divided and fighting. There had been a barrage of memos between the two factions. In numerous department meetings during the past few months, crucial underlying issues of difference were veiled behind superficial discussions of trivia, public posturing, and one-upmanship. Clandestine plotting and scheming occurred behind closed office doors. The opening battle had been over the reappointment of the department chair, but the conflict had then exploded into a full-blown internecine warfare.

As conditions worsened, Mike had unwittingly become an opponent of Bob, a senior faculty member, and Lester, the current department chair. Mike and a department colleague, Richard, had opposed Lester for a second term as chair. Bob, a close personal friend and golfing companion of Lester, had supported Lester's reappointment. Denied tenure at another university for publishing too little and forced to leave academics, Lester had been given a second chance at an academic career by an MU administrator who had previously worked with Lester. Now Lester had been at MU for many years and published little.

Mike had not realized the extent to which Lester would perceive Mike's vote against him in the department chair election as a personal attack on him and his career. Despite a tied department vote and disgruntlement surrounding Lester's first term, the dean reappointed him as department chair. Despite the fact that the vote was supposedly secret, in making the reappointment announcement, the dean revealed who had voted pro and con.

Subjected to increasing harassment, Mike and other opponents of Lester's reappointment began to question Lester's presentation of facts on key department issues. During the next year, the distribution of raises was particularly controversial, because Lester gave the largest raise to his friend, Bob. Mike began to doubt most of Bob's claims of productivity, because he had heard Bob claim he had received more than $1 million in competitive grant funds from national funding sources. Bob had not secured any national funds during his tenure at MU. Normally, academics who receive nationally competitive grants had a track record publishing in peer-reviewed outlets, yet Bob had published nothing in peer-reviewed journals since his arrival at MU and showed an ignorance of research fundamentals.

The controversy over the distribution of raises made Mike and Richard curious to see if Bob had claimed the grant funds on his vita, which they found and read carefully, looking for exaggerations and errors. They found that at least half of the few publications Bob listed on his vita used in his application at MU were nonexistent, or that credit was misrepresented. Mike and Richard saw the false claims on Bob's vita as academic fraud and tried to decide what to do. They knew that the dean who had reappointed Lester would not be anxious to acknowledge his mistake and would likely urge them to ignore the matter, fearing repercussions from Lester's and Bob's supporters. They decided to go directly to the provost with a memo carefully documenting Bob's phantom publications and exaggerated vita claims.

When the dean found out about their memo, he urged Mike and Richard to withdraw their request for a fraud investigation, claiming that such investigation would create further turmoil and dissension in an already fractious department. He said that Bob would likely sue Mike and Richard for damaging his reputation, that Bob's questionable actions were in the past, and that it was best to "let sleeping dogs lie." Mike and Richard argued that Bob's employment based on false claims continued into the present and should be addressed, no matter how much time had passed. They declined to withdraw their request for an investigation of fraud.

After months of silence, the provost called in Mike and Richard to discuss the course of the investigation. He said that things would be tough for them for a while, but they should just hang on while the process ground ahead, because they had unearthed enough evidence to warrant an official inquiry. He said that two little booklets containing faculty procedures pertained to this type of situation. The booklets were vague, stating only that "the appropriate administrator should appoint an investigative body to explore the charges." The provost designated, as the appropriate administrator, the dean who did not want the investigation in the first place.

The dean called up a former chair, Joel, from a related department. Joel's investigation of the case of fraud consisted of meeting once with Bob and asking him about the points in the memo submitted by Mike and Richard. He made no calls nor did he examine other items on the vita, such as grants. Almost 1 year after Mike and Richard had requested the investigation, the dean called them in to report the findings. Joel, the investigator, wrote a four-page report. Two pages said that Bob was sloppy, that information was not presented adhering to academic conventions about attributing credit, and that some facts were misrepresented. The misrepresentations, however, were "inadvertent errors" because Bob had been in a hurry when he prepared his vita for the job application. Joel agreed that the publications Mike and Richard found missing were, indeed, not publications. Nevertheless, Joel concluded that Bob had not committed academic fraud. He said Bob had submitted supporting material at the time he was hired that was more specific on authorship. Joel spent the last two pages of his report chastising Mike and Richard for not simply going to Bob and asking him about the discrepancies they found on his vita. Joel wrote that they should have just asked Bob to produce the supporting material to clarify what he had really done.

Mike was stunned at the outcome and at the investigator's rationale that supporting material compensated for inaccuracies on Bob's vita, or that being in too big a hurry to prepare an accurate vita for a job application was an acceptable excuse. The dean said that, of course, Mike and Richard could continue to press charges at an appeals level, because the faculty handbook provided for another level of hearings, but the outcome would likely be the same. Mike and Richard declined to press the appeal.

Soon afterward, Lester began to retaliate. He wrote to both the dean and the provost, urging that Mike and Richard be fired for "unprofessional conduct." Mike, now disillusioned, and waiting to hear about final approval on a job at another university, spent little extra time in the department and prepared to move.

But behind the scenes, Lester used his position as department chair to intimidate students in Mike's classes into not completing their work on grounds they were not properly trained. He urged them to sign a petition saying their course work was inadequate, and bribed them by promising good grades when they took his sequel course. Only Mike's leaving MU prevented him from being investigated on countercharges of incompetent teaching.

Mike remembered reading articles about whistle-blowers being isolated and exiled from other organizations, but he had never fully believed that the same would happen in a university. Universities were supposed to be run on merit and to adhere to principles of academic freedom and integrity. University administrators and professors were supposed to be guardians of enlightenment, not petty infighters. This ideal was far from his experience the past 2 years. He had been so sure that, because there was wrongdoing, right-minded people would agree it should be addressed. If Mike had remained one more semester at MU, he would have been consumed with fighting Lester over charges of incompetent teaching as well as older department battles. Fortunately, he received a job at another university and left MU. The emotional toll on Mike had been heavy.

Mike discovered that he could not control the behavior of others, and once the dynamics of unethical behavior and conflict are established, they become a vortex that may suck in others. Behaving ethically at all times is a good personal strategy, but if and when others do not, how do you protect yourself? This will be examined in the rest of this book.

2 | The Overlap of Ethics, University Politics, and the Law

Perhaps you think that Mike in the preceding chapter was a victim of poor-performing, ill-willed colleagues and a weak administration. Or perhaps you think Mike "asked for" his troubles and brought the problems he experienced on himself by persisting with his charges against a senior colleague. Whatever your view, no doubt you wish to avoid the situation in which Mike found himself. With skill, strategic choices, and a dash of luck, perhaps you can. The unhappy story of Mike, Bob, Lester, and others at MU illustrates characteristics of ethical dilemmas in universities and colleges. Let us briefly explore those implications.

Characteristics
of Ethical Dilemmas

Ethical dilemmas are emotionally traumatic, no matter what your role in them. Ethical dilemmas are high drama. As they unfold, they grip the participants who often allow the dilemma, its actors, and its resolution to dominate their professional lives. The professors, the administrators, and the students involved become part of a real-life morality play, with real-world implications. Feelings run high and hot.

The panoply of emotions is great across the participants, who may waver between exhilaration over ethical victories and dejection over moral defeat. Those whose actions evoked the dilemma may experience shame and guilt. They fear being caught. Others may be so arrogant they feel no one will discover them, or, if they are discovered, feel no one will dare to do anything about their unethical actions. When caught, they may become angry, belligerent, self-defensive, aggressive, and vindictive.

Those who uncover the ethical violation feel anger, outrage, righteousness, and even revulsion. They grapple with anxiety over whether they should pursue the violation. If they do, others may try to evoke guilt in the pursuers for "turning" on colleagues. They fear and may experience repercussions. Reputations, self-image, and even livelihoods are at stake. Accusations, secretiveness, surreptitiousness, slinking around, and sleuthing cause adrenalin to flow and pulses to race. But the overriding emotions are anger, hostility, deception, fear, and revenge, a far cry from the image of academics as sedate, serene, and cerebral. Welcome to the world of academic ethics.

Ethical dilemmas are more likely in turbulent environments with rapidly changing norms. Ethical values are sometimes reinforced by formal rules. More often, however, their primary underpinning may be informal norms of behavior. In stable environments, norms are relatively constant and change rarely. In turbulent environments, however, norms evolve more rapidly. Standards of behavior and performance may change in a matter of years or even months, not decades. Uncertainty is greater. What is permitted is often not clear in a variety of situations. In turbulent environments, reasonable people may interpret the same event differently, by codes of ethics that have evolved at dissimilar paces and even sometimes down different branches stemming from the same trunk of common custom and experience. Unreasonable people may refuse to adapt ethical codes to changed environmental conditions. Unethical people may use the greater confusion to obfuscate shady actions.

In the case of Mike, Bob, and Lester, standards for performance, particularly in publishing, had been escalating. Faced with this pressure, Bob had altered his vita to appear more prolific than he would have otherwise. Faced with the same pressure, Lester attacked Mike, the prolific researcher who threatened him, more viciously than perhaps he would have otherwise. In a stable environment without escalating performance norms, Bob might have felt less pressure to claim credit for work he did not accomplish. Lester might not have felt threatened and might have muted his response.

Ethical dilemmas frequently overlap with university politics and the law. Ethical dilemmas rarely occur in a vacuum. Instead, as the not-so-nice story above indicates, ethical dilemmas often become intertwined with university politics. Bob's ethical violation went unnoticed and ignored for several years. University politics, not a newly developed desire to be moral cops, caused Mike and Richard to search for evidence of what they increasingly and had already suspected: that Bob typically exaggerated his own accomplishments and performance. Because Mike and Richard had not previously pored over colleagues's vitae looking for misrepresentations, in a less politically charged environment they would have continued their normal practice of accepting a colleague's assertions at face value. A harmonious and well-run department would have resulted in cordial colleagues who were busy doing other things, including their own work.

Threatening lawsuits in these situations show that the ethical dilemmas may sometimes take on a legal dimension. Figure 2.1 shows the relationship between ethics, university politics, and the law. It uses concentric circles to show how ethics—codes of conduct and behavioral norms—affect most decisions and situations. Some subsets of these situations become politicized, for example, situations where political con-

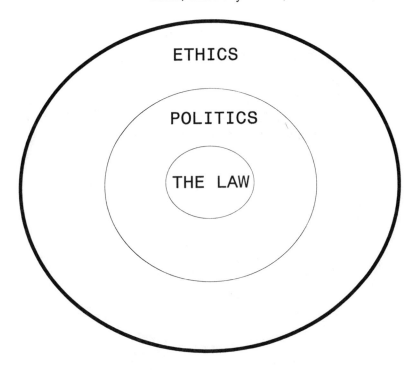

Figure 2.1. The Relationship of Ethics, Politics, and Law

cerns over the distribution of rewards in the university and who gets what become intertwined with ethical issues. In most of these situations, political concerns even dominate ethical concerns both in decision makers' minds and in the outcomes. An even smaller subset of situations is litigated, involving the legal system.

In the peer-controlled environment of academics, most ethical dilemmas are also political. The rich are different from you and I, one author has noted: They are rich. Similarly, university and college professors are different from most other employees in large organizations: Once tenured, they are relatively free and autonomous and without risk of poverty and failure. In theory, they are granted great freedom and autonomy to

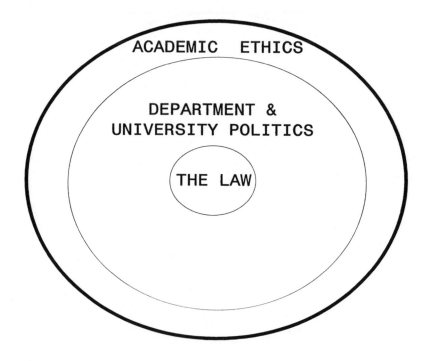

Figure 2.2. The Importance of Political Concerns in Universities

engage in higher pursuits of knowledge development and protection of human wisdom. In reality, freedom and autonomy also allow them to sink to more petty concerns.

University politics about raises, rewards, distribution of funds, perks, and other issues can dominate higher concerns. Tenured professors who spend most or all of their time engaging in politics can do so without financial risk or the threat of losing their jobs. Peer review and governance assure that, under the best of circumstances, legitimate differences of opinion will flower. However, under the worst of circumstances, all issues will be engulfed in politics. Thus, in universities, the peer nature of decision making elevates politics to a larger circle of issues, making ethical and political concerns more closely congruent (see Figure 2.2).

Ethical dilemmas are exacerbated by political fighting. When political infighting erupts, ethical conflicts are exacerbated and personalized, and become very bitter. In our not-so-nice story, questions of who was right and what standards of conduct should be used ultimately escalated to hostility, vindictiveness, and personal attacks on the competence and character of the accusers as well as the accused. When political infighting and factions are overlaid with ethical and moral righteousness, the result can be the organizational equivalent of a holy war. The organization may spin out of control as lines are firmly drawn in support of the accuser or the accused. As the conflict spreads, no one can easily escape its tentacles, and innocent bystanders, colleagues, and students are sucked in as pawns. The purpose of the organization becomes secondary to the battles based on factions that are reinforced with morality and driven by politics.

Administrative procedures for dealing with ethical dilemmas may be weak or poorly defined. Rarely do university policies cover all possible ethical questions. Bureaucratic rules often are developed in response to specific situations, much like case law is developed. In settings where few issues have been debated or anticipated, administrative procedures for dealing with ethical dilemmas may be poorly defined and weak. At MU, for example, the faculty handbook and the book for grievance procedures did not specify who the appropriate administrative officer in any setting would be. Mike and Richard, by initially circumventing the dean, hoped the provost would be defined as the officer. The provost, wishing to avoid having to deal with a potentially controversial and messy issue himself, chose to define the dean as the appropriate administrative officer. The vagueness of the handbook and the procedural manual allowed both interpretations.

In the above case, there were also no guidelines specifying how the investigatory body should be chosen or how many members it should have. Mike's dean chose to pick the investigator himself and to pick only one person, someone similar in background and experience to the accused. The rules for types of communication and what would constitute an investigation were also unclear. Thus Joel, the investigator, could choose to rely only on the verbal testimony of the accused, without any additional input from the accusers other than their original memo or any further investigation on his own part. The vagueness of the official procedures made all these actions possible.

When Mike explored the handbook, there was also nothing in it about faculty elections or ethics violations investigations being secret. Thus the dean's revelations of these matters to interested and third parties did not technically violate official rules. No rules existed. Also, there was nothing in the faculty handbook about the chair of a department urging students to not complete the courses of a fellow faculty member and to draft and circulate a petition condemning that faculty member's teaching competence as Lester did to Mike's students. Such an action struck most faculty as so far removed from any reasonable action that no one had thought to write such a rule or that such a rule would ever be needed. Unusual circumstances, then, are often not covered by administrative rules and procedures, even in well-run places.

Administrative remedies for ethical dilemmas are only as good as the people who implement them. Even the best and most comprehensive administrative procedures can be subverted or twisted if unethical people or those with poor judgment are in charge of their implementation. Administrative procedures and rules cannot dictate that people passing judgment on ethical conflicts be ethical themselves. Rules and procedures may require that more senior people who presumably are more sensitive to prevailing norms be arbitrators of disputes and ethical conflicts. If representativeness across ethnicity, race, gender, disciplines, schools, and other key groups is valued, the rules can require proportional or at least diverse representation. However, rules cannot dictate that an ethical person be placed in charge. Ultimately, high-level university officials up to, and including, the university president and the provost must be in charge of setting the ethical tone. One key way is by the people they select in general as administrators, and particularly to resolve grievances and ethical disputes. This key human decision cannot be written into regulations but, rather, must result from vision and leadership. When it is missing, a well-specified and comprehensive set of rules and procedures to address ethical issues is better than a poorly specified and incomplete set, but an important ingredient is still missing.

The impact of your strategy to deal with wrongdoing may depend on your professional power rather than on how right you are. If institutional procedures for dealing with wrongdoing are not well specified, the impact of any solution you seek may depend on your professional power. It is easier for one colleague to challenge another in a peer relationship than for a subordinate to challenge a superior in a hierarchial relationship. Thus, in theory, a professor can challenge another faculty member of the same rank more readily than a department faculty member can challenge a department chair or a dean. Tenure provides additional protection to both challengers and accused, when pitted against an untenured faculty member.

Although in our story, Mike was challenging a fellow faculty member, Bob, Bob augmented his power base by relying on his personal friendship with Lester, the department chair, to seek retaliation, converting what would have been a challenge within a peer relationship to a hierarchial challenge. Lester was inclined to rally to Bob's rescue to the extent possible, because Mike had also failed to support his chair renewal bid. Although hierarchial challenges can on occasion be won, victories are often less frequent and at greater costs.

Whistle-blowers pay high costs, especially when they are right. Whistle-blowers and others who press for the resolution of an ethically based conflict may find that the costs for doing so are considerable. In Mike's case, he was subjected to a barrage of countercharges, from attempting to wield undue influence on the investigation of Bob's record to charges of incompetence in teaching and overall. The costs emotionally were high. Whistle-blowers may become distracted from professional work and suffer productivity gaps or declines. Other costs are being labeled a troublemaker and isolation from colleagues.

Untenured whistle-blowers may lose their jobs. Tenured faculty may not have the same concern about losing their job, but Mike's case shows that tenure is not an absolute protection. Mike was tenured, but tenure did not protect him from charges by Lester that he should be fired because of incompetent teaching. Nor does being right about the charges whistle-blowers make necessarily protect them. Being right may even exacerbate the anger of those who side with the accused. Further, investigations into charges that whistle-blowers bring rarely result in clear-cut decisions. Often the outcomes of such investigations are muddy, and what wrongdoing means is subject to interpretation. Bob was indeed found, for example, to have listed nonexistent publications, but the investigator chose to interpret the listing as an excusable "error."

The ultimate club in an ethical dilemma is the law and the pursuit of legal remedies. Legal actions are the course of last resort, to be used for someone grieving an action after internal remedies and appeals have been exhausted. Legal actions are a powerful club, once wielded sparingly, but now wielded more frequently as American society becomes more litigious. Even the threat of a lawsuit can alter behavior. Few university administrators hate any word more than the dreaded one, *lawsuit*, especially if the suit is filed against them or the university while they are in charge.

Parties in a whistle-blowing episode can also threaten to sue each other. As Lester's behavior showed, even those without personal standing to sue can urge direct parties in a whistle-blowing encounter to sue. The dean used reports of this to attempt to quell a formal inquiry into Bob's misrepresentations. Lawsuits and threat of lawsuits in a worst case scenario, except for the lawyers, can become a free-for-all, with everyone threatening to sue everyone else. The modern showdown at high noon has moved from the "O.K. Corral" to the "O.K. Courtroom," with legal missives substituted for bullets.

Threats of lawsuits will eventually lose their potency unless, at some point, the threatener follows through. Mike, for example, had heard Lester threaten in impassioned outbursts to sue various people on past occasions. Although toward the end, Lester claimed he has sued three colleagues on previous occasions and won, Mike knew of no lawsuit he had initiated while at MU. Many university administrators, however, have become so lawsuit shy, they do not wait to find out if the threatener is firing blanks.

University administrators are often more concerned with minimizing conflict, establishing a smooth-functioning process, and avoiding lawsuits than with the outcome of any particular ethics violation case. What would have happened had Mike remained at MU? Would not the higher officials at the university have intervened? Because Mike left, the answer is not clear. Probably, the provost and the dean knew that if Bob's tenure had been revoked he would have sued the university. In such settings, where one outcome is termination of a faculty member, removing that person may be less important to administrators than "fixing the process" to avoid replicating the error. By selection and nature, administrators often wish to avoid conflict and to promote harmony to keep their units functioning smoothly. Proactive procedural changes will be of greater importance to them than retroactive remedies in any particular case.

Several books in the **Survival Skills for Scholars** series provide useful tips on how to handle ethical issues in particular settings. For example, can professors be too easy or too tough in their grading and testing practices for purposes of self-interest instead of the students' interests? This issue is discussed in *Tips for Improving Testing and Grading* (Ory & Ryan, 1993). Walter Gmelch (1993) addresses techniques for dealing with stress caused by the trauma of an ethical dilemma in *Coping With Faculty Stress*. Ethical approaches to improving teaching strategies and techniques are described in *Improving Your Classroom Teaching* (Weimer, 1993). Benjamin Bowser, Gale Auletta, and Terry Jones (1993) look at discrimination and favoritism in *Confronting Diversity Issues on Campus*. Some ethical issues in the crucial career point of tenure and the role of university and departmental politics in decisions about such issues are discussed in *Getting Tenure* (Whicker, Kronenfeld, & Strickland, 1993).

Plan of the Book

The rest of this book examines ethical dilemmas in greater detail. The book is divided into four parts. Part I has raised the question of the importance of ethical dilemmas to all involved, including you if you uncover a wrongdoing. Even when you are not the perpetrator, ethical dilemmas that are poorly handled can derail your career. The power you hold within the academic institution as well as how right you are may impact on how you will be affected by raising an ethical dilemma.

In Part II, we examine what constitutes ethical dilemmas in university and college settings. We explore four different categories of dilemmas. Chapter 3 considers dilemmas concerning faking publications and credentials, lying on vitae, and questions of who should take credit. Chapter 4 looks at dilemmas surrounding fraud in research, whereas Chapter 5 considers the issue of sexual harassment. Chapter 6 briefly examines "fuzzy ethical issues" where the nature of the issues involved is more ambiguous and consensus about how to approach the issues is less clear-cut.

In Part III, we look at how to stop ethical violations. We aim here to give you strategies for coping with dilemmas that may arise in universities and colleges. Chapter 7 identifies and examines the advantages of various strategies you might pursue, up to and including whistle-blowing. This chapter focuses on informal strategies. Chapter 8 looks at formal strategies for addressing ethical violations, including using the administrative grievance process and the courts.

Those of you who walk in the land of the ethically aware and wary will find this book useful in ruminating about past episodes as well as preparing for any future dilemmas you may confront. Undoubtedly, some of you are idealistic or skeptical that you will ever need such information. Reality, however, will likely prove otherwise, for if you have never experienced an ethics-related conflict, the probability is great that at some point in your career you will. And if you do not, you are truly in the promised land with a chosen few. This book is written for the many who are less lucky.

PART II

What Are Ethical Violations?

3 | Faking, Lying, and Taking Credit

Are your colleagues who they say they are, and have they done the things they claim to have done? Most of the time, the answer is yes, but what should you do if you suspect otherwise? This chapter addresses questions of fake credentials, falsified degrees, and phantom publications. We also explore here nettlesome issues about who should take the most credit for research, and sometimes, who should take credit at all. The case of Nan illustrates that issues in this area are not always clear-cut, and opinions about the appropriate outcome may lack consensus, even when agreement emerges that an ethical violation has occurred.

Proving the Dissertation Is Done

Nan was a young, ambitious academic with a good career under way. She had a large number of publications based on her dissertation and was now involved in several major collaborative research projects with two different groups of colleagues in her current department. She worked long, hard hours and expected to be considered for tenure early. Over the past 2 years, she had experienced many moments of doubt about some aspects of her colleagues, but she knew that as an untenured assistant professor she needed to keep working.

So what if one of the collaborators (along with her department chair) got drunk a lot. As she was learning, this happened in many departments. The problems with another person were harder to ignore, however. She was convinced that he had lied about completing his doctorate. Recently, she realized that he may even have fudged research results. What should she do? And how did she, a person who believed in honesty and hard work, get into this situation?

The story began several years before the situation described above. A major midwestern state university with a medical center created a new health-related program. A small unit of five faculty was created. With promises of eight new hires, the faculty in the new unit were happy and enthusiastic at first. Nan was especially pleased, because she had transferred internally from another department. She felt her opportunities for research and publication would be enhanced. All the newly hired younger faculty felt that the types and amounts of research they would do or might do in this setting could help their careers. Everyone was committed to the new unit and anxious to progress. The new department chair was the happiest. He loved to build departments and would be able to do what he liked best: build a new unit and energize faculty and students alike.

Herbert, the chair, eagerly started planning for hiring of new faculty. He drafted potential job descriptions, which he gave to the faculty to go over them. In the areas of Nan's expertise, he already had two faculty members, Nan and Keith, a relatively young associate professor. His plan was to recruit one junior person in Keith's field and another more senior person in a related area. There were many outstanding candidates for both positions. One young associate professor, Paul, currently on the faculty of one of the best universities in his field, was recruited for the more senior position. Herbert and especially Keith were even more enthusiastic about Jim, the new person hired in the junior position. Jim was in the process of completing his doctoral degree with one of the best known experts in the country. His references were outstanding, and, at his interview and presentation, he impressed everyone with his quantitative skills.

When the next academic year began, the department was a place brimming with enthusiasm and commitment to work hard. New graduate students had been admitted. Five new faculty were in place. Everyone got to work designing the curriculum, teaching new courses, and beginning new research projects. Nan quickly became involved with two research teams. One involved Paul and other colleagues in the medical center who had ongoing projects that were going well. She also became involved in several projects with Keith and Jim.

This new work team initially appeared harmonious because the work required complementary skills from all three team members. Keith, the most senior of the three, handled internal politics. Jim and Nan were involved in every phase of the projects, including designing the overall research plan, writing research proposals, training students and interviewers to collect data, and analyzing data on the computer. While awaiting funding for major projects, they used starter funds to begin small projects. As junior faculty, Nan and Jim put in long hours, working days, nights, and weekends on data collection, coding, analysis, and writing.

As the year progressed, Nan became concerned that Jim was not finishing his degree. Keith and Herbert were also concerned and kept pushing Jim to get it done. Nan tried to talk to Jim as a friend and a fellow junior faculty about the need to finish. At first, he talked with her about what was left to do. Then, increasingly, he became angry when she raised the issue of finishing the dissertation. She backed off. In spring, she was relieved when Jim announced that he was through and was going back to his university to defend his dissertation. He was gone for a week; on his return everyone congratulated him, and a party was organized to celebrate. Jim changed the articles and grant proposals being submitted to indicate that he was a Ph.D.

Nan was pleased that the issue was resolved, but surprised. They had worked so many hours together over the past 6 months. She found it hard to believe that Jim had found more hours in the week to complete his dissertation. Only a few months before, he had been discouraged during their conversations and had indicated that he had a substantial amount of work left to complete. Nan thought about the issue a bit and decided to leave any skepticism aside. Despite the behavior of her colleagues, both her teaching and research were going well. She did not want to upset things.

In the next month, she was at a professional meeting and saw Jim's major professor, Dr. Kline. She had never met him but decided to introduce herself as Jim's colleague. When she did, he made one brief comment to her; that is, that they really needed to be sure that Jim was given time to finish his dissertation. Nan was now quite confused and unsure what to do next. Should she tell Keith or ask Jim directly? A call to the registrar at Jim's old university indicated that Jim was still being carried as a graduate student and had not received his degree that spring.

Nan was now even more worried. They had just sent off articles and a grant application listing Jim as a Ph.D. She did not want this inaccuracy to come back and be used against her. Finally, she decided to tell Keith about her conversation with Dr. Kline. At first, he said she must have misunderstood. She said she was fairly confident of what he meant, but perhaps Keith (who knew Kline), or Herbert, the department chair, should call Dr. Kline.

During the summer, she and Jim continued to work on projects. Several times she asked him when he would send off articles from his dissertation, mentioning her own last two articles from her dissertation data set. She watched his reaction closely. He said his dissertation had less potential for publication than the current projects. One evening, they were working at the computer center, trying to finish results in time to meet deadlines for an abstract for a meeting. Tired and hungry, Nan agreed when Jim encouraged her to go home while he finished the work. That next morning, Jim had a draft of the abstract for her to see. It had new results that looked encouraging. She excitedly asked to see the runs, but Jim said there was no time because she needed to shorten the abstract to fit into the required space. After it was ready for mailing, she again asked to look at the results and thought of a new twist to the analysis to try in a few days. Jim said he had inadvertently thrown out the results when cleaning up from the mad rush to get the abstract out.

At home that night, Nan began to worry about whether the data runs had really been completed. Because she was now convinced that Jim had lied about completing his degree, she now trusted him less on all other aspects of their joint work. As the summer progressed, she continued working with Jim and Keith, and with Paul on other projects. She grew more and more concerned about Jim's ethics. A similar issue of producing results for an abstract happened again at the end of the summer. Moreover, neither Jim nor Keith were following up on the degree issue. Nan finally confided in Paul and included the information that she had called the registrar. Paul was furious and called Dr. Kline. Jim had never finished.

Nan was glad the degree issue was out in the open but felt the brunt of Keith and Jim's anger, damaging their working relationship. Keith became upset when she insisted that they write the journals where articles were pending to change Jim's degree status. She did not want to be caught having participated in the lie.

When it was time to reapply for a grant that Jim, Keith, and Nan were on, along with Herbert, the department chair, Herbert left her off of the project. Herbert said Nan was not a good team player. She was furious and arranged another meeting with him. They exchanged several memos, each growing angrier and angrier in tone. By the end of the month, Herbert made it clear she was now viewed as a troublemaker. Nan realized that, despite having been correct on Jim's lying about his degree (and possibly about his faking some of his results), she was now the one in trouble. Over the next year, she applied and interviewed at a large number of universities and landed a comparable position, but at the cost of having to change positions and cities and disrupt her family. Jim ended up being appointed as an assistant professor, even though he never obtained his Ph.D. degree.

Analysis

What are some of the relevant lessons and important issues raised by this story? What were the other options Nan had when she discovered that Jim had lied about the completion of his degree? There are probably a range of situations connected with lies about credentials and claiming of credit in research efforts. The situation in which proof is usually the easiest to obtain is that of faking degrees or credentials. Proof about claims on a curriculum vitae (CV) can also often be obtained, but not as easily or as simply. Least clear-cut are the ethical dilemmas that occur about who gets credit for work, listing of authorships, and inclusion or exclusion of names on publications. These are discussed in the last part of this chapter. Another whole range of ethical dilemmas in research concerns the conduct of the research itself, and those issues are discussed in the following chapter.

In the past decade, a number of stories about faked credentials in various fields have occurred. Many universities now require a transcript to be submitted, documenting that a formal degree has been awarded. If Nan's university had required a letter from Dr. Kline at the time of the defense of the dissertation, some of Nan's problems would have been solved. Therefore, whether you are a new or a more senior faculty member, one lesson is to require formal verification of the award of degrees. A young faculty member should not feel insulted if this is required, because it eliminates any future questions.

How else might Nan have handled this situation? Nan tried to deal with the uncertainty of whether Jim had received his degree informally and internally, through hints to Jim himself and by talking with other faculty members. Jim ignored the hints, and Nan was convinced that a direct confrontation would not work. She could have ignored the lie and not have disrupted relationships with her colleagues, but this both offended her sense of appropriate norms and ultimately placed her in danger of being seen as a collaborator in Jim's deceptions (which in truth she would have been). Her problems would have been fewer if the first faculty member to whom she confided her doubts had taken action or supported her taking action. Should Nan have taken a formal action such as writing a memo to the chair? Nan had strong reasons to believe that the department chair, Herbert, did know about her suspicions. If that was true, she would have needed to involve the dean and the vice president. She probably could have undertaken a formal appeal also, having challenged Jim's right to his appointment based on falsification of degree. In the case of someone lying about a degree, a situation in which it is fairly easy to determine the facts, it probably would not be necessary to move to external strategies, either informal ones such as peers and media or formal ones such as professional associations or the courts, because there is wide agreement that one should not claim falsely to have a degree, and proof of whether this is true or not can often be simply obtained.

Avoiding Lies and Inaccuracies

How can you avoid ethical issues surrounding lying on vitae that Mike in Chapter 1 and Nan in this chapter confronted? Several tips are described below.

1. *Be sure you cannot be accused of lying on your own vita.* Outright fabrication of untrue events and achievements on the vita may be less common than "padding" the vita with exaggerations and extensions of partial truths, but both are wrong. Be sure you cannot be accused of such actions. Within academe, your CV becomes the public record of what you have done and your accomplishments. Although it should represent you well, to avoid ethical dilemmas, it is critical that it represent you accurately.

2. *Revise your vita if expected publications do not occur.* Be careful about placing articles on the CV as publications until you have the formal letter from the editor. If the journal ceases publication before your article comes out or the publisher reneges on a book contract, be sure to delete these references from your CV so that no one can accuse you of inaccurately pumping up your CV. Similarly, be careful about putting the order of authors correctly on your CV. You do not want to give someone else the opportunity of claiming that you lied. Unlike Bob, the accused in the story in Chapter 1, whose colleagues rallied to his defense, you might end up providing someone with "proof of lies" through being careless.

3. *Retain a copy of each published article.* One part of advice that is especially important for untenured faculty is to be sure to retain a file with at least one copy of each publication cited on your CV. If anyone questions one of your publications, you can then easily produce the written proof. Many universities now require that a copy of each publication (and perhaps even of each paper listed as submitted or presented at a meeting) be included as documentation to back up a tenure and promotion file to verify the vita at this critical stage of an academic career.

4. *Check out items on the vitae of others if you begin to suspect a problem.* Another aspect of accurate vitae is to be sure that CVs of others are accurate, especially if you have reason as in the example in Chapter 1 to distrust a colleague. Before accusing someone of this, try to obtain the most recent copy of their CV, and thoroughly check out all the citations. Be sure your charges are accurate before you make them. Although the issue of lies on a CV is not as clear-cut as lies about degrees, it is usually possible to verify the claims on a vita. Thus internal remedies are likely to be successful, although as the story in Chapter 1 illustrates, it is often hard to prove "intent" to lie and deceive. If the internal remedies fail, as they did in the story in Chapter 1, external remedies of telling peers and appealing to ethics committees of professional associations (or even the courts if you can prove direct harm) are possi-

bilities. Such approaches will generally escalate potential conflict (particularly to a level of visibility beyond your own university) and thus this may increase the chances of negative consequences to you.

Sharing Credit

The situation of sharing credit and apportioning credit across various researchers in a field is a research situation that often results in interpersonal difficulties and questions about fairness. One reason these occur is that standards differ across fields. If people never worked in groups, there would be few issues of sharing credit. The reality in today's larger research universities is that in certain fields one almost never works alone. This creates a host of situations related to sharing of credit. In humanities fields, it is still common for people to work alone or at most in pairs. In contrast, in biological, chemical, and health sciences, most work is done in larger groups, often in the lab of the senior professor. This is less true of theoretical work in those fields. In social sciences, there is more variability. Because norms vary, you must understand your field and your institution. The most complicated situations may arise when people work across disciplinary areas.

One good (and often difficult) example of ethical dilemmas in sharing credit occurs around a student's dissertation research. In the field of political science, the association published *A Guide to Professional Ethics in Political Science*. This guide states that "as advisors, faculty members are not entitled to claim joint authorship with a student of a thesis or dissertation" (American Political Science Association, 1991, p. 10). This norm may also seem appropriate in many humanities fields. But in many science areas or social science areas in which large amounts of money and/or time are needed to collect new data, it is common for doctoral students to work on a portion of their professor's funded research as a doctoral dissertation. They work in the professor's lab or analyze data from a larger project. In these situations, the publications from a dissertation often include the entire research team, although the first author should be the doctoral student.

Norms often change over time. Within the health care field, for example, there has been discussion over the past 4 years of a need for all authors to have been active participants in planning the research and conducting the research and article, not simply having been participants in data collection at one stage or in the collection of clinical data. To assure that everyone is aware of the manuscript and to deal with issues of copyright, many journals now require a form to be signed by each author listed on a publication. A few journals even require a letter of submission of the article to the journal to be signed by each author at the time of initial submission of the article.

Discuss issues of joint publication at least briefly at the beginning of projects. Because norms differ across fields and because determining who did the most work on a project is not easily verified, many difficult ethical situations can arise over sharing credit. You should try to avoid becoming embroiled in such situations. No one strategy works for all situations. If possible, discuss issues of joint publication at the beginning of a project. Try to understand how authors will be ordered, so that the person who writes the first draft will be first or the senior investigator will be first on the first three articles.

If there is a clear understanding initially, problems are less likely to develop later. If you agree to one approach, you have to be willing to stick with it throughout the project. Thus it is important initially to be collegial, but to avoid being treated unfairly. Not every detail can be worked out in advance, however, and trying to get too specific can often in itself lead to problems. Some smaller research groups may rotate first authorship to avoid potential fights over ordering. In the past, a strategy in some fields was to list authors alphabetically with a note that this was the approach employed. Many journals object to this approach, however, and it is actually less fair than a rotation rule because some sources of citations list only the first author and the citation type in many journals gives greater prominence to the first author. A person with a name at the end of the alphabet would inadvertently and consistently receive less prominence and always be penalized.

Be sure all authors see articles before they are mailed for review. Increasingly, journals require some indication that all authors have seen the article and have approved the final version. This can help to avoid surprises among team members over taking credit. When disagreements do occur over taking credit for a project, they often can be very bitter. Establishing who did the most work or who did not do enough work to continue to be included in publications from a project can be very difficult to prove. Having agreed on credit assignment prior to submission of an article helps to prevent the issue from blowing up into a major external controversy.

If a dispute becomes more formal, it is generally difficult to arrive at a clear ruling from formal mechanisms, either from an administrative or grievance strategy internal to the university or from external grievance procedures in an academic disciplinary association or a court. Administrative rulings may occur, however, as a way to resolve conflict among colleagues in a project. Because these types of disputes deal with one of the critical aspects of academe, publication and receiving credit for scholarly work, one certainty is that disputes about credit and ordering of authorships, although not uncommon, end up reflecting poorly on all those involved. If at all possible, professors and researchers maintain their own reputations by working out such disputes internal to the project, or to the smallest academic unit involved.

Remain sensitive to disciplinary differences. Disputes are more likely to occur in interdisciplinary research. If one field respects multiauthored articles more than another, issues of sharing credit take on additional importance. Although often people working together are from units with similar norms, this is not always true. Norms may vary about both the number of authors and preferred journal outlets. Being aware of the different norms can sensitize research team members to each participant's own career needs.

Be aware of the political aspects of credit issues. Most ethical issues rapidly assume a political dimension, affecting the allocation of resources and the potential for conflict. Whether the ethical dilemma involves lies about credentials, lies about accomplishments as reflected on a CV, or lies about the amount of work and effort involved in a project and the publications resulting from it, they are emotionally traumatic, fueling political conflict. Even in the clearest cases (those involving lies about credentials), being right does not always correlate with coming out on top. As you move to more ambiguous situations, rules to deal with the problems become less clear. The likelihood of factions developing increases and situations become more and more political, although politics and lack of fair application of administrative remedies can occur at any level, as illustrated in the story at the beginning of this chapter. Academic ethics is a broad issue, but in universities and colleges most ethical issues quickly become political ones as well.

4 | Fudging Research and Related Scholarly Sins

Much scholarly and academic research takes place in a secluded, private arena, with no one checking to verify the correctness of the data or material the researchers used, or indeed, even whether they conducted the research at all. Yet out of this environment of many people working separately or in small teams independently, with little or no supervision, emerges knowledge. The knowledge is presumably generated systematically, painstakingly, incrementally, and often slowly. However, it has profound implications for modern living.

In such a decentralized setting, trust is most important. Others must trust that what researchers and scholars say to be true is indeed true and that what they say did not happen failed to occur. Accuracy is highly important. Sloppiness is not acceptable. A scholar and a researcher are only as good as their word. If the valued and valuable trust is ever shattered, reputations and careers are also shattered. Rarely can tarnished trust be restored to its original luster. Yet countervailing pressures also exist—pressures to produce results, fast and now. Within modern research laboratories, whole cadres of people depend on the senior scientist for their own well-being.

Scholars in other fields may be tempted to quote directly or excessively from the work of others to meet manuscript and publishing deadlines. These countervailing pressures sometimes overpower the pressures for trust and accuracy, with unhappy consequences for all.

Haste Makes Waste

Initially a young and enthusiastic scientist, Adam felt he would end up with a tenure-track appointment at a major university, such as the prestigious midwestern university to which he had just received a postdoctoral appointment. He wanted to have a successful academic career, a huge accomplishment for someone from his background, coming from a family in which no one else had even graduated from college. From high school on, his willingness to work long hours, his intense interest in science, and his intellectual curiosity had marked him for a type of academic success he had never imagined at the beginning of high school. But none of his college success had prepared him for his current situation— working with someone he increasingly distrusted. How did he get caught in this situation? More critically, how could he get out of it?

Only 3 years ago, he had been elated over a postdoctoral appointment at a well-known university, working in the laboratory of a famous researcher, Dr. Barrow. His major professor, David, had warned him that, because the lab in which he was going to work was huge, he would probably work under the supervision of one of the assistant or associate professors, not Dr. Barrow directly. Internationally known, Barrow traveled frequently and left much of the details of his research to his large group of associates. Adam had enjoyed the smaller lab and the warm and friendly research relationship with David, but he was ready to move on to a bigger challenge. He felt lucky to attain such a prestigious postdoctoral appointment, especially because his degree was from a reasonable but not outstanding program.

During the first year, Adam had worked long, long hours, of course—a given for a postdoc in a prestigious lab. He was initially assigned to a project well under way with a senior assistant professor, Karen, who was supervising the work. Despite the time commitment to the lab, he was able to complete the publications from his dissertation as well. Karen had a good grasp of work in the lab and was a careful and meticulous researcher. By winter he helped conduct the analyses and writing for several articles about the new projects, resulting in him getting coauthorship. He felt his career was getting off to a good start.

Adam's only disappointment about the year was how little contact he had with Dr. Barrow because Dr. Barrow was gone so much. Adam had only talked to him a few times. In one of those brief talks, Dr. Barrow spoke positively of a recent acceptance of a paper from Adam's dissertation, and of what good things Karen said about him. According to the other postdocs, this was great praise, although it did not fully compensate for the loss of the personal conversations, family dinners, and picnics he had shared with his former mentor, David. He now appreciated what an unusually friendly and warm relationship David had provided for him. Still, overall, it had been a good year. The next one looked promising as well.

After the first year of his postdoctoral appointment was completed, Karen suggested that Adam begin to think about new projects with funding sources separate from the postdoctoral program. She reminded Adam that his postdoctoral appointment was only for 2 years. He needed to think about looking elsewhere for a tenure-track appointment. With Karen's encouragement, Adam talked with Chet, one of the associate professors, about one of Chet's projects related to Adam's dissertation. Working with several of the faculty might increase his chances of staying on as an assistant professor. While continuing to work on Barrow's projects, Adam began to prepare a smaller grant proposal with Chet as the principal investigator to submit to their professional association re-search fund.

This led to a collaborative effort on a conference paper with Chet as the senior author. Chet worked differently than Karen and David, who both spent long hours in the lab and kept thorough, detailed books of lab notes. Chet had become impatient at one point when Adam wanted to redo one result and check results in the lab book. He was impatient to get the paper off for a meeting deadline and then revise it for publication, so Adam gave in.

With only 6 months left on his postdoctoral program, Adam began to worry about his future and talked to Dr. Barrow, who knew Karen might leave. Dr. Barrow said that, if Karen did leave, it would open a tenure-track slot to give to Adam. If not, he would let Adam stay for a few years on a research assistant professor grant-funded position. Dr. Barrow had heard about Adam's budding romance with Ann, a graduating doctoral student, and said he could save a postdoctoral slot for her. Whether Karen left or not, Dr. Barrow indicated he felt Adam should work more with Chet.

Adam was thrilled at his luck. He would have a tenure-track position, could get married, and Ann would have a post-doctoral appointment. The next week, Chet and Adam heard their smaller grant was funded. Everything was going right, even though Karen announced within a month that she would leave. Spring zoomed by. Ann completed her dissertation, and Adam gradually shifted more of his work to Chet's projects. As he worked more and more with Chet, he realized he had little in common with him. Chet liked to live well, and he wanted Adam and his postdocs and doctoral students to keep up with the details. Given Dr. Barrow's schedule, Adam now realized that Chet was a major investigator on almost all the grants, especially with Karen leaving.

Over the summer, Adam had many papers to complete for meetings. Chet traveled part of the summer. As Adam worked away, he started to have trouble finding all the lab books and data from the experiments. Moreover, on several of the papers, as he repeated the experiments, he could not get the results to match those in the abstracts accepted for the meetings. In fact, a whole set of material was completely missing. As he talked to one of the postdocs, he began to hear stories about how quickly Chet worked at times and how he would run some research in his smaller private lab. Adam became more and more worried. He was not sure the research had been done correctly, yet he had to finish the papers by Chet's return. He decided he needed to talk to Chet and find the missing materials when Chet returned.

On Chet's return, Adam asked for more complete details and to see some of the lab books. Chet said he did not always keep the kind of detailed records Karen had and that Adam would have to get used to it. When Adam discussed the problem with numbers not matching on one project, Chet laughed and agreed to use Adam's numbers at the meeting. Adam finished the papers, and they went well at the national meeting.

The next year was more difficult. Because Adam was now in a tenure-track position, he was teaching. This took more time than he had expected. He could not be in the lab as much as he wanted. As work began on the new grant, Chet and Adam clashed over the pace of the work. Adam wanted to be sure everything was right. Chet wanted to meet the work schedule. As a report came due, results were not yet finished. Chet said he was sure how they would turn out and they needed to send the report off. Adam wanted to ask for an extension or to write up only their limited progress. Chet sent the report, and implied results were finished.

Adam was upset. He felt this was almost faking data. He then remembered his last year's inability to find lab books or to match numbers. Was part of Chet's work faked? He started asking the postdocs and the doctoral students. Everyone had a few instances of problems, but both postdocs warned Adam to think through what he was saying. He had no real proof. As Adam and Ann talked at home, he realized he had to talk to Chet about his concerns over missing data and nonverifiable results. He did so the next day in as nonconfrontational manner as possible. Chet got angrier than Adam had ever seen. He said Adam would never make it in the competitive world of science today if he did not learn to take shortcuts and be quicker. The conversation escalated. Adam directly accused Chet of cheating at times. Chet got madder still and told Adam he wanted him off his projects. He would speak to Dr. Barrow on his return. Did Adam not realize that Chet now had a huge reputation, linked to Dr. Barrow?

Even before Dr. Barrow's return, the department and lab were in turmoil. People chose sides. Most sided with Chet. Adam quickly made an appointment with Dr. Barrow. He decided to write down his suspicions, as part of a memo to Dr. Barrow. During the next week, Chet told Adam to move his separate projects out of Chet's lab and that they could no longer work together on new projects. The issue of joint papers would be left to Dr. Barrow to decide. Adam's meeting with Dr. Barrow went poorly. Dr. Barrow had already talked to Chet and believed his story. He told Adam he was making serious accusations with no real proof, thus jeopardizing both Chet's and Barrow's reputation. He handed the written memo back to Adam, suggesting that both Adam and Ann would be better off at a different university in the fall. If this issue were dropped, however, they would obtain good references.

Adam and Ann agonized over what to do and decided to send his memo to the dean. Within a week, the dean called him. He told Adam he had no proof, noting that Dr. Barrow had generously agreed to help place both of them if they would quit spreading rumors. Adam said these were not rumors and that he might submit a formal grievance. When the dean responded by suggesting a meeting with university lawyers present, Adam knew things were out of control.

For advice, Adam called both David and a former postdoc now at another university. Both were alarmed for Adam. The friend suggested giving in, but knowing Adam better, David realized Adam was convinced that Chet was behaving unethically. He suggested Adam see a lawyer before he talk to the university lawyers, advice that Adam followed. The university lawyers wanted Adam to sign an agreement not to raise these issues with anyone outside the university. In return, both Adam and Ann could continue at the university and would each be paid their salary for the next year if they did not locate new positions. Dr. Barrow would provide letters of recommendation if the agreement were signed. Adam could not bring himself to sign the agreement, filing formal charges instead. The next month, at a professional meeting, he told many people the story. Word got back to Chet, who threatened Adam with a personal lawsuit. Dr. Barrow made it explicit that Adam and Ann must leave by fall and that he would not support their hunt for new positions.

Adam and Ann applied for a number of more research-oriented positions at various universities, but rumors had spread that Adam was difficult. Some even had heard rumors he faked data, getting the stories confused. No offers came. His old mentor, David, finally called and offered Ann a post-doctoral position in his lab and a 1-year sabbatical replacement position for Adam. In the next year, David convinced them to drop the internal appeal against Chet and to tell Dr. Barrow they would not repeat any more stories. David used his contacts to find each of them an assistant professor position at two smaller colleges, only 40 miles apart. Their academic careers continued, but not in the high-powered arena of science Adam had once hoped for.

Options for Dealing With the Situation

Although Adam and Ann managed to salvage a career in academe, it was not the high-powered scientific research career Adam had once planned. Moreover, if David, his doctoral advisor, had not continued to care about his former student and first arranged temporary positions and then helped them find permanent positions, Adam's career in science might have been over. What could or should you do differently if you found yourself in Adam's position? There is not a simple solution.

If Adam had been willing to convince himself there were no problems with Chet and his research, he might have stayed on at his position as an assistant professor. Or, once having raised the issue, he could have landed in a more similar type of academic position if he had been willing to accept the initial offer of Dr. Barrow. Given that he believed there to be serious wrongdoing, what else might he have done?

In retrospect, confronting Chet at all may have been a mistake in this case. Once Chet talked to Dr. Barrow first, Chet was believed. Perhaps if Adam had talked first to Dr. Barrow and indicated how concerned he knew Dr. Barrow would be given his outstanding reputation and their shared commitment to high-quality science, Dr. Barrow might have believed him and talked to Chet in a different way. Although internal, informal measures may often be the best way to begin, this may not be the case on a charge as serious and potentially career ending as scientific fraud and faking of data. In this case (as contrasted with inaccuracies on a vita, which, although serious, probably will not end a career), talking to the administrative authorities first might have been better or might not have, depending on the extent to which Dr. Barrow had any inkling of a prior problem.

As happened in the story above, university administrations often side with more established investigators. Adam was not in a strong enough position to buck Chet alone. Perhaps if he had talked with others first and a whole group of postdocs in the lab were also willing to discuss problems with Chet's work, the outcome might have been different. As a group, they could have raised questions with the National Institutes of Health's (NIH) office, overseeing scientific wrongdoing without as serious repercussions for any one of the questioners' careers. Perhaps, but most likely, others would have been frightened of losing their own positions.

As this story demonstrates, internal grievance mechanisms are slow and work poorly for people in vulnerable positions in academe (such as a postdoc and an untenured assistant professor). If Adam had been a tenured associate, he might have been able to ride out the controversy and pursue internal grievances, to file a charge with the NIH, and perhaps to obtain justice. Often, especially in science, but even in other fields where collaboration is less typical, it is the junior person who may observe questionable research approaches on the part of a senior person. If the situation is reversed (for example, a faculty member detects a student falsifying data), the power relationships and administrative system are much clearer, and the student is likely to be forced to leave the university. Power differentials matter. Typically, the senior investigator will be believed unless there have been prior reasons for administrative leadership to doubt the senior person's research performance and honesty.

If both formal and informal internal procedures do not work to expose wrongdoing and to protect the person noticing the problems in the case of research fraud, what does work? To some extent, Adam did try external informal strategies by talking to his friends and to a broader circle of colleagues at the meeting. However, he did not try a media or overall publicity strategy. Although talking to his close friends, and especially his former mentor, David, was critical to salvaging a career, these approaches did not expose the wrongdoing of Chet. Moreover, the use of the external strategy of talking at one of the meetings, given the differentials in the participants' status in the field, probably hurt Adam and made other places unwilling to hire him. Ideally, Adam would have been able to collect hard evidence that Chet was cheating before making accusations. Adam might have fared better personally if he had kept the information to a very tight circle of friends until after obtaining another position and then pursued an external, formal approach through his professional association or some other group such as the NIH. In fact, for untenured junior people, probably the best advice once research fraud is suspected at one's institution may be to try a simple talk with the department chair or the head of the lab or research group. If that person dismisses the idea of problems, back off and look for a different position without talking more except to very close friends or mentors. Once safely at a new position, a junior person can decide whether to pursue external approaches if the evidence is solid. A deeper discussion of these strategies appears in Chapter 7.

Issues of Scientific Wrongdoing

Differences in Wrongdoing by Field

Perceptions of what constitutes scientific wrongdoing vary by field. The above example fits best for the biological and physical sciences and health science centers, in which people typically work in teams. With some variation, the story could be true in a number of social science areas as well, where people may work together on first gathering data and then analyzing a large data set. Faking lab results might not be detected, but similar issues of faking data, throwing out aberrant cases, or changing numbers in data tables and analyses could occur. We have probably all heard some rumors of such behavior.

Faked data and other science-related concerns have received increased attention over the past 5 years in the pages of *Science* and in *The Chronicle of Higher Education*. Recently, a panel of experts was assembled by the National Academy of Sciences to deal with the issue of ensuring integrity of the research process (*Responsible Science*, 1992). These sources provide a more detailed discussion of aspects of these controversies. Also, the Office of Research Integrity (ORI) within the Division of Research Investigations at the NIH is now both more active and more public in its actions than it was before. The ORI was established on May 29, 1992 to replace a differently named office with some similar responsibilities. It participates in investigations of scientific misconduct brought to its attention, involving studies using NIH funding. This office is now be a major place to which suspicions such as those of Adam could be brought.

This branch of the NIH now publishes the final findings of scientific misconduct in various issues of the *NIH Guide for Grants and Contracts*. This is the type of mechanism Adam wanted to find in his case—a way to alert the entire field to the misconduct. For example, the issue of June 25, 1993 ("Final Findings," 1993), published the names and paragraph type descriptions of wrongdoing by 14 different investigators. Generally, those found guilty are barred from receipt of funds for some period of time (varying depending on the seriousness of the incident) and then are required to submit special certifications for some future period of time for any work submitted. In some of the cases, published papers have also been retracted. Many of these investigations have taken a number of years, however, so that the cautionary notes about being in a more secure position and away from the institution in which the problems are occurring before raising the charges and prompting an investigation are still appropriate cautions in many cases.

Plagiarism

In the humanities and some of the social sciences such as history, plagiarism is more often the dispute equated with falsification of research. Stealing ideas from colleagues can occur in humanities, and in social and natural sciences. A number of recent controversies about plagiarism have achieved prominence, and discussions about ways of detecting such instances have increased. Some of these discussions involve renewed national effort and attention to detect fraud in research and scholarship. Other prominent examples have involved the efforts of the NIH in detecting plagiarism.

What is plagiarism? In 1989, the American Association of University Professors (AAUP) issued a formal statement on the obligations of professors as regards plagiarism. That statement defines plagiarism as "taking over the ideas, methods, or written words of another without acknowledgement and with the intention that they be taken as the work of the deceiver." The statement continues discussing other aspects of plagiarism and points out that even within the academic community, there are complexities and shades of difference. One example of a famous person and possible charges of plagiarism within the academic setting involves the case of the doctoral dissertation of the Reverend Martin Luther King. Although accepted by Boston University at the time without any issues being raised, some recent researchers on King's life have pointed out the similarities of phrasing, and paragraphs to, other published sources. Defenders of King have argued that, in the oral tradition of ministers, and especially of Black ministers, words are often repeated without direct attribution. As this controversy demonstrates, outside of academic settings, definitions of plagiarism are even less clear. This was also illustrated in the controversy a few years ago about Senator Joseph Biden of Delaware using portions of a speech made by another politician without attributing those words.

Whole books have been written on plagiarism (LaFollette, 1992), and this chapter cannot cover all the details and intricacies of the issue. One point of confusion and difficulty is evident in the AAUP definition. A portion of that definition emphasized that plagiarism includes situations in which the intention of the author is that the words be taken as his or her own, not as those from another source. Intention, however, is notoriously difficult to prove. This is one of the difficult aspects of many plagiarism cases. Was the intent to deceive? Were the citations merely too careless? What is such a common phrase or idea that no citation is needed? How much material must be similar and how similar must it be without proper citation for there actually to be plagiarism?

A case involving a historian at the University of Massachusetts, Stephen Oates, received great attention and illustrates both the difficulty of defining plagiarism and of using "more scientific" approaches to determine if it occurred. This case was complicated with the effort by the NIH to establish standards about ethics and accuracy in research. Oates is a well-known biographer, having published life histories of

Abraham Lincoln, William Faulkner, and the Reverend Martin Luther King, Jr. Since 1990, he has been accused of plagiarism in the biographies of all three people. The most recent accusations are linked to two investigators at the NIH, Stewart and Feder (Magner, 1993; Wheeler, 1993). Earlier, five different academics had filed complaints with the American Historical Association (AHA) about Oates's work. Oates's defensive stance was aggressive as he threatened litigation and accused others of having ulterior motives (Magner, 1993). The controversy also involved the use of a "plagiarism machine" by two NIH scientists to determine if Oates plagiarized (Wheeler, 1993). The plagiarism machine is computer software that searches different documents for identical phrases, a new approach to reviewing claims of plagiarism.

Earlier, the AHA investigated the claims against Oates and issued an inconclusive report. Although the AHA did not find plagiarism in the case of the Lincoln biography, they did "conclude that his Lincoln book was 'derivative' of a 1952 book by Benjamin Thomas and that Mr. Oates 'had failed to give Mr. Thomas sufficient attribution' " (Magner, 1993). As some other historians who have defended Oates have pointed out, he generally writes about well-known public figures for whom little new information is unearthed for a new biography. However, even some of his defenders argue that he has been careless in his use of composition.

Complicating the issue is that Oates was not accused of lifting entire sentences or paragraphs, but rather of plagiarizing a large number of short, descriptive phrases, making the use of a plagiarism machine appropriate. How the two scientists, Stewart and Feder, got involved in the case is itself controversial. Although the two have studied plagiarism and scientific misconduct at the NIH, they do not work in its investigative office. They sent a large package to Oates by Federal Express containing a letter accusing Oates of plagiarism and demanding a response to a 1,500-page communication contained within. A very short deadline was given, with a response demanded in only 1 day (Wheeler, 1993). Oates, after a brief period of panic, became outraged because he had no current federal grants and did not understand why non-historians should be evaluating his work in this manner. He protested to Senator Paul Simon, also an author of a biography of Lincoln, about the NIH investigators' allegations and the way in which they raised their charges with him. He also filed a formal complaint against Stewart and Feder. The final conclusion to this investigation has been closing the laboratory in which Stewart and Feder worked and their reassignment to separate and new responsibilities within the NIH. Without making any judgment of the accuracy of any of these claims, this case nicely illustrates the difficulties that whistle-blowers can have themselves, especially in cases where proof is hard to find and truth thus hard to determine. Similarly, Oates's reputation has been sullied again, without any additional determination of the veracity of the arguments beyond the AHA report.

Protection of Human Subjects

The issue of the protection of human subjects has received special attention for many years. Thus rules are more clear-cut, and issues of how to establish violations are routinized. At least within most disciplines where applications for federal funds are common, all investigators understand that certain procedures must be followed. Although researchers often complain among themselves about the complexity and the time delays these processes introduce, violations of the procedure are most infrequent. The receipt of federal funds requires that universities certify special procedures for research involving human subjects. Many disciplines have codes that cover such conduct.

Most universities now have well-established systems for protection of human subjects, because such assurances and committees are required for the award of federal funds. At any university, you can easily find out the application process involved to have research that includes human subjects reviewed by the appropriate committee. The rules and specifics are well spelled out, and there is usually a staff member and always a faculty member who chairs such a committee available to provide further information. Although there are a number of complexities about issues of human subjects, they are not the types of ethical violations being dealt with in most of this book and they will not be reviewed further.

Politics and Research Fraud

Again, as in the case of lies about credentials and CVs, ethical dilemmas about research, falsification of data, and plagiarism all can quickly escalate and become emotionally traumatic. Cases in these areas are often even less clear-cut than in the case of lies about credentials. The fuzzier "the truth" in any given situation, the more political the situation is likely to become and the more important relative power differentials within the unit are. Overall reputations also become important. There are increasing ways that questions about inappropriate conduct can be raised with an outside group such as the NIH as well as professional associations in many disciplines, but the consequences of whistle-blowing remain. In many cases, individuals are better off raising questions once they have moved to a new institution or are in a quite secure position in their current institution.

5 | Sexual Harassment

Lust, Confusion, and Abuse

In recent years, concern has grown over the ethical dilemma of sexual harassment. The Supreme Court confirmation of Clarence Thomas led to a televised clash between him and former Equal Employment Opportunity Commission (EEOC) employee and then University of Oklahoma law professor Anita Hill over Thomas's behavior toward Hill while acting as her supervisor. Hill charged that Thomas had sexually harassed her by repeated advances and crude language and behavior. Thomas countercharged that Hill had delusions about a relationship with him and was showing the enmity of a woman scorned. The nation chose sides between the two. As both were grilled by an all-White male panel, women throughout the nation vowed to run for office and hold the reigns of power, kicking off "the year of the woman" in politics. Of course, sexual harassment had gone on before the Thomas hearings and would continue afterward. But most important, the nation's consciousness about sexual harassment would never again be the same.

Sexual harassment refers to unwanted advances and conduct typically experienced as offensive in nature made in the context of unequal power or authority (Friedman, Boumil, & Taylor, 1992). Sexual harassment includes verbal behavior of a sexual nature, unconsented touching, and requests for sexual favors. Due to the nature of power relationships in the workplace, the perpetrators have mostly been men in a position of authority who are able to threaten the victims' jobs, promotions, or employment benefits. In universities and colleges, the perpetrator may be a professor and the victims may be students.

The courts first recognized sexual harassment in 1977 as action violating Title VII of the Civil Rights Act of 1964. Before 1977, the problem was largely ignored as a private matter, not one deserving of a public policy and organizational policy solution. Subsequently, EEOC guidelines have broadened the definition of sexual harassment to include three qualifications or conditions that produce it (Cole, 1990). First, sexual harassment is unwanted sexual advances, requests for sexual favors, and other verbal or physical conduct of a sexual nature when submission to such conduct is either explicitly or implicitly a term or condition of an individual's employment. Second, sexual harassment occurs when submission to, or rejection of, such conduct by an individual is used as a basis for employment decisions affecting such individual. Both of these types of harassments are called *quid pro quo harassment.* Third, sexual harassment exists when the sexual conduct of another has the effect of unreasonably interfering with an individual's work performance, or of creating an intimidating, hostile, or offensive work environment. This condition is called *offensive environmental or condition of work harassment.* In 1993, the U.S. Supreme Court in a unanimous decision broadened considerably the proof allowed by a plaintiff to prove a hostile working environment. For definitions of sexual harassment, see Table 5.1.

What should you do if you are confronting a situation where sexual harassment occurs? You may find yourself in the awkward and unpleasant situation of being personally harassed. Although women have been the predominant victims in the past and heterosexual men the perpetrators, men are not immune from harassment. Men may be harassed by other men, and increasingly, as women achieve positions of power, they also may become harassers. What do you do if you observe a colleague or administrator harassing someone

Table 5.1 Sexual Harassment Defined

Sexual harassment
Unwanted advances and conduct, typically experienced as offensive in
nature, made in the context of unequal power or authority.

Basis in federal law
Title VII of the 1964 Civil Rights Act dealing with employment.

EEOC[a] guidelines identifying conditions of sexual harassment
Quid pro quo harassment
When submission to the sexual advances or demands of another is
either explicitly or implicitly a term or condition of an individual's employment.
When submission to or rejection of such sexual conduct by an individual is used as a basis for employment decisions affecting that
individual.
Offensive environment harassment
When the sexual conduct of another has the effect of unreasonably
interfering with an individual's work performance, or of creating
an intimidating, hostile, or offensive work environment.

---

[a] EEOC = Equal Employment Opportunity Commission.

else, likely students who feel less powerful and may be para-
lyzed in knowing what to do? Following are some points and
tips for dealing with sexual harassment.

The law is now on your side. Remember if you become embroiled in a case of sexual harassment that the law is on your
side. As in the case with drunk driving, public attitudes have
changed during the past few years, to become aware of the
problem of harassment and to no longer automatically assume
that a person who is harassed "asked for it." Even if your immediate co-workers are not supportive of your complaints of
sexual harassment, the law is on your side. A court case,
Vinson v. Taylor, has found that employers are liable for allowing a substantially discriminatory environment (Cole, 1990).
This heightens the stakes for all involved in a case of sexual
harassment and increases the likelihood that college admini-

strators will pay attention to any such charges. Even a single incident of harassment is now considered sufficient to bring a charge against an employer.

Discuss the situation with sympathetic friends. If you are being harassed and trying to decide what to do, discuss the situation with sympathetic friends. You may discover that the perpetrator has harassed others and that you are not alone. Sexual harassers have developed an attitude toward power and their freedom to use it inappropriately to obtain sexual gratification that likely has been developing for a long time and may persist even if you succeed in curbing unwanted advances. This underlying attitude increases the likelihood that the harassing behavior is a habitual or long-standing one and that others have been harassed as well. If this is the case, and you join in action with others, your case is much strengthened.

Even if you do not discover that others have been harassed, talking with close friends is useful for two reasons. First, you will likely need the emotional support, as being trapped in a power relationship where unwanted physical interaction is being pressed on you is highly traumatic. Second, your friends can later corroborate the timing and circumstances of your concerns. Be careful, however, in the early stages in whom you confide. You do not wish to be accused of spreading unsubstantiated rumors about colleagues.

Discover whether or not your college or university has a sexual harassment policy and what it is. Most colleges and universities now have moved to adopt sexual harassment policies and guidelines. Your first step if a problem is brewing is to find out from either the EEOC officer or the personnel officer if there is such a policy and what it is. What are the formal steps for addressing a case of sexual harassment? Knowledge is power, and in any future confrontation with the harasser, knowing the official policy may jolt the perpetrator to the reality that he is engaging in a serious offense.

Make clear that the sexual advances are unwanted and offensive.
Initially, you may have been flattered or at least not offended
by any special attention the perpetrator showered on you,
especially if he is powerful and has significant control over
your career. You may have thought that the attention was
being directed to you for your work performance and that
it indicated you were bright and capable. Perhaps you only
became uncomfortable with the situation as it became increasingly sexual in context and substance. Perhaps you even
were initially attracted to the perpetrator, but only became
uneasy as the situation advanced rapidly, you discovered
personality characteristics in the perpetrator you did not like,
and the power implications became obvious. It is important
that, if you are feeling harassed and pressures, you clearly
state you want the unwanted behavior to stop and not send
out mixed signals.

*Make plain to the perpetrator that you want to maintain cordial
working relations on a nonsexual basis but will seek relief if his
behavior is not changed.* In an attempt to keep good working
relationships with the perpetrator, try discussing the problem
with him in a nonthreatening way. You might say that, although you enjoy working with the perpetrator and wish to
continue to do so, and respect his professional accomplishments and expertise, you are increasingly uncomfortable
with the growing sexual nature of your interactions.

Depending on the situation and your assessment of the
character of the perpetrator, you may or may not give reasons. The more reasons you give, however, the more you limit
yourself and are forced to justify your own legitimate prefer-
ences as if they were illegitimate. If you say that you do not
wish to become involved with someone at work, you preclude yourself from then easily forming a mutually consen-
sual relationship with a colleague at any future point. If you
say you do not find the perpetrator appealing, he will surely
be offended. If you say you do not want a relationship now,
the perpetrator may contend that he is surely the only one

who can overcome your reluctance and problems. Most likely, the perpetrator will be married, as many in positions of power in organizations are.

Your best strategy here is to provide little information about your motives, except that you wish to maintain friendly, cordial working relations and that the increasingly overt sexual advances are straining that valuable professional tie. Firmly state that you do not appreciate nor want the sexual advances but do value professional advice in work-related matters. Your success in using this strategy depends in part on the character of the perpetrator. If he is someone who has just slowly across the years strayed over the boundaries of what is acceptable and appropriate, you may jolt him back to reality. If, however, he is someone who enjoys the abuse of his power, this strategy may not work and you may even become the object of retaliation.

Keep a journal of all unwanted interactions, the time, and the content of each. If sexual advances continue, start keeping a written record of their content and timing. This will later be important if you decide to pursue institutional and official remedies. Carefully document all the crucial aspects of the unwanted advances, including where and when they occur as well as who is the perpetrator. It is better, after referring to your journal, to be able to say that "in the third week in July in the copy room, there were three unwanted encounters of this type," than to just say that "Professor X harassed me."

A written record of this type will be useful in demonstrating a pattern of harassment. Also keep a record of any sharp reversal in decisions affecting your welfare that occur after your rebuff of advances. Detail the date and timing of such retaliatory efforts. To the extent possible, detail the lack of performance rationale for it, leaving only retaliation for rebuffing the perpetrator as a plausible explanation. Because most harassment occurs when no other parties are present but the harasser and his object of harassment, often sexual harassment charges boil down to an issue of who is more credible:

you, the accuser, or the accused perpetrator. Because by the nature of harassment, the perpetrator is likely to be more senior and powerful, it is important that you maintain good records to mitigate any countercharges that you are acting arbitrarily, capriciously, or maliciously. Such a record will also help mitigate the common countercharge that you initiated any sexual interaction and that now, having been spurned, you are retaliating by making sexual harassment charges.

Realize that inappropriate sexual advances in more diffuse settings than the chain of command may require other remedies. The definition of sexual harassment pertains to the immediate workplace. Although you may be able to extend it to include nonhierarchial relationships that do not impact directly on your career under the "hostile environment" definition of harassment, doing so may be difficult. Consider the case of Jill, who served on the tenure and promotion committee at her university. The chair of the committee, Bill, a powerful scientist on campus, became attracted to her and began to come on to her as the days of long and intense meetings passed. At the end of the meeting, the chair arranged for the entire committee to meet at a local bar to celebrate the conclusion of most of the year's work. At the bar, he became increasingly sexual, sitting by her, and eventually rubbing her leg with his hand under the table. As the party broke up, he followed her back to her office, wanting to get together that night. He said that he had had an understanding with his wife and had affairs with graduate students and colleagues in the past. She contended that she had other plans.

Across the next few weeks, troublesome cases were discussed over the phone, including one in Jill's department. Earlier during the meetings, Jill had argued strongly to delay one case that had insufficient evidence for tenure and to overturn another decision that seemed political to her. These cases were ones for which she had had primary responsibility to review. In both instances, Bill had supported her enthusiastically, and the committee had unanimously supported Jill's position.

As weeks passed, Bill repeatedly called to "get together," and Jill was consistently busy. To retaliate, Bill, as chair of the committee, asked Jill to come to his office to pick up a file for an appeal, and then made her wait for an hour and a half for it. In another instance, Bill called Jill and told her that the decision on the two controversial cases under her initial review had been reversed. Jill was dismayed. Bill claimed he had some secret information too confidential to reveal. However, he had called a majority of the committee members on the phone and convinced them to reverse their decisions. He had not bothered to call her because he knew she would oppose it.

Jill went to two vice presidents in the university to complain about the handling of the cases. She revealed to the woman vice president her perception of the underlying dynamics. Although sympathetic, the vice president did not suggest any remedial action. Then Jill went to the provost. Because Jill had no proof that the reversal of the cases was in retaliation for her sexual rebuffs, she did not raise the sexual harassment dimension. She knew both the provost and the committee chair had been on campus together more than 25 years and knew each other well. After all, the provost had appointed Bill to head up the important universitywide committee. Rather, Jill complained about inappropriate procedures. She argued that reversing a case outside of a formal meeting with no written record or transcript violated due process and fairness. The provost agreed, but nothing happened and the cases remained reversed.

Jill was emotionally drained and felt violated by her interactions with Bill, even though her own career had not been appreciably damaged, other than to be perceived as a troublemaker by university officials. In her mind, sexual harassment and retaliation had occurred but her immediate career was not at stake. She saw no way to raise the issue of sexual harassment. Although she was not successful in reversing the decisions on procedural grounds, the strategy of attacking the consequences of sexual harassment in this diffuse non-hierarchial setting was more realistic.

Avoid any appearance of sexual harassment yourself. It is important to avoid any appearance of sexual harassment. One way to do that is to avoid any sexual or romantic relationships with anyone—colleagues or students—at work. Such a strategy, however, has never been adhered to, as male professors with regularity have dated and married former students. How the relationship began varies by situation. In some instances, the relationship leading to romance and marriage plainly began while the student was still in a degree program in which the professor taught. Recently, at least one higher education institution, the University of Virginia, has considered adopting a policy forbidding all romantic or sexual linkages between faculty and students, no matter whether the professor personally supervised or taught the student. Most universities, however, have not adopted such stringent rules. Rather, in most settings, there are informal norms that professors should not date students currently taking their classes or over whom they have significant supervisory responsibility. Implicit norms have also emerged that dating older or more mature students who are adults is less exploitative than dating traditionally aged college students who are less experienced and, in theory, more vulnerable. However, age differentials are only one factor in determining whether or not a relationship may take on exploitative overtones.

Regardless of the official policy of your university, you are well-advised to try to keep your personal romantic and sexual life separate from your work life, especially from students over whom you have implicit, if not explicit, power. Your primary role as a professor when interacting with students is to be a teacher and intellectual mentor. If you are personally looking for reinforcement from students for being attractive, lovable, and emotionally and sexually appealing, you have created a role conflict. A romantic relationship requires reinforcement to go both ways. In an intellectual mentorship and teaching role, you are responsible for nurturing the mental development of those junior to you in status or development. The demands of the two roles may collide; you are being paid and are given public trust to be the teacher, not the lover. At times, if you are an energetic and concerned teacher, students may develop a crush on you. The temptation to become involved, especially if the student is attractive, bright, and strongly attracted to you, may be great. However, in most settings, the best solution is to rechannel the students' interest into the intellectual development they need and are in college to get, without hurting their feelings. Students grow up, leave the university, and become happy productive adults, if they have learned and developed well under your tutelage. That is the time to become involved, if you are still so mutually inclined.

Do not ignore complaints by students who contend they are harassed. Students may be reluctant to discuss harassment by professors and may require great courage to try to talk about inappropriate behavior with someone else. If a student comes to your office for advice or for some other reason and in the course of the conversation reveals inappropriate behavior by a colleague, do not ignore it. Encourage the student to go to the student counseling center and to write down the offending behavior. If a professor is abusive of students, rumors may circulate for some time to that effect before an incident blows up, becoming public and controversial. If you become involved, however, be aware that university administrators may have differing proclivities to deal with sexual harassment. Some administrators do not want to see the problem and prefer to ignore it.

Consider the case of Gail, who worked in a modest-sized department at a state school with both graduate and undergraduate programs. Rumors had circulated for some time that the department chair, Frank, a married man, dated students and used department fellowships to implicitly bribe students into accepting his sexual advances. These rumors had reached the dean on several occasions, but lacking hard proof or any angry student confronting him, the dean chose to ignore them as unsubstantiated. One day, an undergraduate student appeared in Gail's office and said that Frank had propositioned her and had promised her a graduate fellowship and to set her up in an apartment if she would consent to being his lover. The student said that she had been making an A in Frank's course, but when she refused this arrangement, she then was given a C for the course. Gail encouraged the student to go to the dean. Again, the dean ignored the complaint and did nothing. The student, with Gail's encouragement, filed a suit in federal court for sexual harassment. Now the dean listened, as he was named a party in the suit. Frank, sensing that Gail disapproved of his behavior and was counseling the student on seeking remedies, became vindictive toward Gail. On two occasions, she went to the parking lot and found her tires slashed. Frank was forced to take a leave of absence and disappeared from town as the case became more controversial. His wife filed for divorce. Eventually, the university settled with the student, and as part of the settlement, Frank, who was now working at another college in another state, resigned, with tenure revoked.

Encourage your university to educate students about sexual harassment policies and remedies. Official sexual harassment policies at your college or university should include a program for educating students about the issue and what remedies they have if they experience it. Undergraduate students in particular may benefit from such an educational effort, although graduate students may also benefit. Undergraduates may be less aware of options and how to deal with the problem. Graduate students, however, having selected a career and now involved in a program where the personalities and their performance may impact greatly on their career chances, may have more at stake in any clash with a major professor. Empowering students to deal with sexual harassment, as well as educating professors about its potential negative impacts on their own careers and on students, are all approaches for dealing with this ethical dilemma.

6 | Dealing With Fuzzy Ethical Issues

Some possible clashes over campus ethics involve "fuzzy" ethical issues—where norms of behavior are less clear-cut than in the areas of lying about professional accomplishments, faking research results, and sexual harassment. In these areas, standards for conduct are evolving, ambiguous, or both. Fuzzy ethical issues include questions of conflict of interest, some student-related issues and peer review issues, and concerns surrounding recruitment.

Fuzzy Ethical Issues

Conflict of Interest

Conflict of interest is just beginning to receive detailed attention, particularly within universities. The rules and procedures in these cases are less established and less well specified than for protection of human subjects discussed in Chapter 4. One recent controversy may best illustrate the types of issues that can occur. A common type of health care problem for children is an earache caused by an ear infection. One of the leading researchers in the area has been a scientist at the University of Pittsburgh and Children's Hospital. During the past 11 years, he has received more than $12.5 million to study ear infections and related problems (Cordes, 1993). This group of researchers has been supportive of the use of antibiotics to treat the condition. The main researcher from the group, Dr. Bluestone, has received about $50,000 a year in honoraria from the pharmaceutical industry, typically for speeches paid for by drug companies. The director of research for Bluestone's department, Dr. Cantekin, became concerned about papers drafted by Bluestone and other researchers, believing that they overstated the effectiveness of antibiotics in these situations. Cantekin wanted to publish a paper with a different interpretation of the data, but Bluestone objected. Cantekin complained to the NIH about possible scientific misconduct. The NIH investigated and did not find substantial evidence of scientific misconduct but was concerned about the amounts and frequency of the honoraria. In December 1990, Bluestone and his staff were placed under a special supervision arrangement with the NIH for 5 years.

Yet somehow a close associate of Bluestone, Dr. Stool, was awarded the guidelines project to develop rules on how doctors should treat the ailment, funded by a different federal health agency, the Agency for Health Care Policy and Research (AHCPR). This agency did not realize the previous controversy, and the NIH now claims that it did not tell the AHCPR because no wrongdoing was ever determined (Cordes, 1993).

The other difficult aspect of this case remains the situation of Cantekin. The situation is not simple, and Cantekin and Bluestone became involved in a dispute over authorship of a paper and other issues as well, leading to an investigation of Cantekin by both the university and the NIH. What happened to Cantekin? To reinforce the point that being a whistle-blower is not fun or easy, he is currently on probation at the university for 5 years (Cordes, 1993).

The debate over conflict of interest and appropriate rules to deal with such situations remain unresolved at most universities. The example above raises at least two major questions about conflict of interest: What is an unacceptable conflict of interest in federal research and reviews? How can government protect against bias, given that many scientists are linked financially with companies involved in the area or receive some type of corporate support as well as federal support? One way to prevent conflict of interest would be to prohibit any contact between researchers and industry groups that use the research for commercial ventures. Instead, the trends in science and other research areas are going the other way. Especially within health and science research, because the NIH and the National Science Foundation (NSF) budgets have not been increasing as rapidly as the rate of inflation during the past 20 years, the search for alternative sources of research funding has increased. Joint ventures with private industry are one solution. As joint ventures increase, the situation may become even more complex, as the Bluestone case illustrates. Moreover, it is not clear that Bluestone violated any rules because, although the University of Pittsburgh requires disclosure of conflict of interests, it does not prohibit receiving honoraria from business.

This is one of most ambiguous areas of academic ethics. For an individual faculty member, what do you do if you suspect conflict of interests among others? How do you avoid them yourself? In many federal situations now, such as the evaluation of grants, formal statements of lack of conflict of interest are required of members of peer review panels. One way to avoid all situations of conflict of interest is to not to engage in consulting work, at least not with for-profit corporations, that could potentially benefit from aspects of the research. Yet many professors find consultation an important source of additional income, as well as useful at times for research ties. (See Robert Metzger's [1993] *Developing a Consulting Practice* in this series for greater details on this topic.)

Rules about consulting are not the same at all universities. Particularly at state universities, some may allow a great deal of consulting, including the establishment of private companies headed by the university faculty member, whereas other states prohibit university faculty members from heading a private research corporation. One important guideline is to find out what the formal written policies are at your university about both consultation and submission of grants to private foundations. Know what the policies are and follow them.

Student-Related Issues

Ethical dilemmas may arise over how to treat students in various situations. Exactly how close, for example, should you become with students? Plainly, sexual harassment is wrong, but what about becoming good friends in a relationship that may not be sexual in character? At some point, do your expectations as a friend clash with your duties as a teacher and mentor? Proximity to professors facilitates learning from them and, indeed, is a college characteristic that both parents and students may value. But too much proximity may become suffocating, and a conflict may arise with a need to maintain a sufficient distance to motivate and evaluate students. Situational and often delicate decisions are required to determine appropriate behavior.

Some professors may also exploit students to meet their own research concerns. Although involving students in your research projects as either subjects or assistants in data collection may sometimes provide insight into how research is conducted, when does doing so deviate too much from established curriculum expectations and what students need to know? Generally, the more advanced students are, the more they can benefit from exposure to the research process, but again, no hard norms of right and wrong exist.

Does using your own book as a required text in a course you are teaching constitute exploitation? If you have written a popular textbook that has been widely adopted at many colleges other than your own, obviously not. If you have written a research monograph that is quite expensive and appropriate only for the most dedicated scholars in a narrow subfield, obviously yes. But most questions about using your own book fall somewhere in between these two extremes.

Peer Review Issues

Other fuzzy ethical issues involve the peer review process. Supposedly, reviewers are "double-blind" anonymous—they do not know whose work they are reviewing, nor does the author of the reviewed work know who does the review. But subfields are sometimes small, and if you are an active researcher, you may know many of the ongoing major projects being conducted in your area, and others may know of your work. In such instances, the assumption of anonymity may be violated.

What should you do if you receive a manuscript to review and you can identify the author from the subject and style? Should you refuse to review the piece? Should you tell the editor and let him or her make the judgment call about whether you should review it? Or should you keep your recognition of the author(s) to yourself and proceed to review the article as fairly as possible? The smaller the subfield, the greater the likelihood that you were selected to do the review because you had the requisite knowledge and background that someone less familiar with the area may lack. Although many scholars would argue that you should at least inform the editor of your recognition, not everyone would agree.

Another peer review issue is whether you as a reviewer should reveal your identity to those whose work you have reviewed. You may share common research interests and through your reviewer activities identify others with whom you might discuss research issues. Some scholars would contend that you should wait until the reviewed work is in print so that the anonymity of the review process is preserved. But the time delay between the acceptance of a piece and when it actually appears in print can be considerable, and what if the reviewed work is rejected? Others argue it is OK to get the editor to reveal your identity to the author or authors of the work and give them the option of contacting you. Again, no hard and fast norms exist.

Recruitment Issues

Recruitment for new hires and other opportunities has always been plagued with issues of cronyism and discrimination. Each involves letting a preconceived bias alter your judgment. In the case of cronyism, your friendship and emotional ties to a candidate, or to a sponsor of a candidate, may tempt you to push for hiring that person, even though other more qualified people are competing. In the case of discrimination, prejudices against a particular group may result in you resisting the hiring of someone. Because all searches and hires involve some judgment calls about who best meets the criteria, proving this type of unethical influence, especially undue cronyism, is difficult. However, both issues remain ethical dilemmas within the academy.

Strategies to Avoid Being Accused

How do you avoid being accused of improper behavior in dealing with an ethical dilemma? Not all situations involve you accusing someone else of wrongdoing. Some—especially fuzzy ethical issues where standards of behavior are less clear—may involve others accusing you. Obviously, you wish to avoid such accusations. Several strategies are available to help you. Each strategy has advantages and disadvantages.

If in doubt, do not do it. The advantage is that caution before the fact is better than regret later. The disadvantage is that, if other people are "doing it," you may be at a competitive disadvantage.

Perhaps the best precaution against being accused of unethical behavior is not to do anything that could be perceived as unethical. Caution before the fact is better in most instances than regret later. To gain maximally from this strategy, you should avoid not only the actuality but even the appearance of impropriety. Yet several problems may prevent this from being an effective strategy in any particular setting. First, you may want to do "it," and you may be at a professional competitive advantage if you do not. For example, if others are consulting extensively and using the contacts to gain access to research monies and practitioner communities, you may be disadvantaged if you do not consult also, even though questions of conflicts of interests may arise. Second, if someone is intent on accusing you, ethical conduct on your part will not prevent them from doing so. Well-intentioned actions can be twisted in interpretation, or false accusations may be levied.

Check with friends. The advantage is that friends are likely to be concerned about your interests and understand your background. The disadvantage is that friends talk with other friends who talk with still more friends.

Friends are likely to be concerned about your interests and to understand your background and current circumstances. If you are pondering whether an action is ethical, check with friends first. If your friends conclude it is unethical and you will look bad, your enemies will draw the same conclusion more quickly and you will look worse. Friends, especially experienced, savvy friends, are a good reality check. Of course, the disadvantage of this approach is that friends may talk with someone unfriendly who interprets your contemplations in the worst possible light.

Check with department colleagues. The advantage is that department colleagues understand the department personalities, norms, and politics. The disadvantage is that department colleagues may be more concerned about their own position in the department than about yours.

Although friends may be more concerned about your interests, department colleagues may better understand the department and university personalities, norms, and politics. Thus their advice may be more pertinent in any given setting.

Department colleagues, however, may also be personally caught up in any particular situation and may not have an unbiased perspective. Moreover, department colleagues who have never worked in any other university or college, or only in those of different character or of lower quality than the current institution, may not give well-founded advice either.

Check with your department chair. The advantage is that your chair may have particular information germane to your concerns. The disadvantage is that, if your chair receives a negative impression of you, he or she is in a position to influence your rewards and raises.

If you are concerned about the ethical implications of some action you are contemplating, you might check with your chair. This, of course, assumes you have a cordial working relationship with your chair. If you do not, this option is precluded. And, if you are going to do whatever you are contemplating anyway, checking with the chair may be risky. What if the chair urges you not to pursue your planned course of action? Not only are you now in the situation of being perceived as engaging in questionable behavior but you are doing so against the direct advice of your chair. There is an old saying "Never ask for permission to do something if you know you plan to do it anyway." It applies here.

Check with peers elsewhere. The advantage is that peers elsewhere have a different institutional perspective. The disadvantage is that peers may not understand key particulars about your college or university.

If you do not have colleagues with whom you can express genuine concerns in your own college, turn to friends at other colleges and universities for advice. Peers elsewhere have the advantage of having a different institutional perspective, but they may not understand fully key particulars about your college or university.

Strategies to Use When You Are Accused

Despite your precautions to avoid being accused of unethical behavior, this unhappy and traumatic event still may occur, especially in areas where ethical standards are fuzzy. Being innocent of the charges does not necessarily reduce the trauma but rather increases your own sense of outrage and of being treated unfairly. Several strategies exist for dealing with this distressful state of affairs.

Keep a file on the episode and keep all memos. The advantage is that later some memos may be hard to find and events may blur if you do not have a written record. The disadvantage is that memos do not capture private conversations or some events and may include posturing that is not obvious to a disinterested reader.

It is very important to keep all memos and other forms of documentation concerning the charges. Months may pass as the case unfolds. Given the amount of paper involved in teaching, conducting research, and service commitments, retrieving key memos may prove difficult if you have not filed them away. Further, without these key memos to jog your memory, events may blur, or you may forget details. One disadvantage of this option, however, if your file of memos becomes your official record of the charges and the events surrounding them, is that formal memos do not capture private conversations or some events. You can address this somewhat by writing a memo after every key meeting to recap and confirm what was said. Another disadvantage is that memos may include some posturing among the parties that are not obvious to a disinterested reader. Key issues may be obfuscated. To the extent possible, write responding memos clarifying true intent and underlying issues. Memo writing is a true craft, one that you should develop extensively if you are accused of unethical behavior and wish to survive. In the end, he who writes the last memo has the last say. (See Arthur Asa Berger's [1993]

Improving Writing Skills in this series for help with writing effective memos.)

Write a memo to the file when there is no other written documentation of a salient event or discussion. The advantage is that this allows you to keep an "official" record of verbal and other events not covered in memos exchanged among the parties. The disadvantage is that writing lengthy and comprehensive memos is very time- and energy-consuming and entails opportunity costs.

In some instances, it may not be appropriate or to your advantage to send a memo to a colleague or university administrator, particularly if that person is your adversary. However, you may wish to record negative encounters and interactions in such a way that you will have a written record of them should you need it. In these instances, write a memo to your file. This may be less official than one actually sent, but nonetheless provides a coherent written sequence of transpiring events to someone unfamiliar with your case learning about it by reading the written documentation. This includes an appeals or grievance board or a lawyer reading about your case. A disadvantage of both this strategy and the first strategy of keeping and responding to memos is that memo writing takes time and energy away from productive activity. In very bad situations, it can consume most of your efforts.

Avoid being alone with the accuser or any close friends of the accuser. The advantage is that this reduces the probability the accuser will be able to distort what was said. The disadvantage is that, depending on who the accuser is, you may not always be able to have a third party present.

In an adversarial setting when you discover that a colleague or university official is accusing you of unethical behavior, you may be tempted to charge in alone and confront the accuser. Do not do so. Avoid being alone with the accuser or any of the accuser's close friends. Conversations with no witness and no tape recorder can be distorted and statements can be fabricated. In short, your accuser can lie about that as well as your initial behavior. Yet lies with a kernel of truth are more believable than those that bear no relationship to reality. It is easier for an accuser to lie about what you said if you are meeting alone with him than if you never meet alone. A disadvantage of this strategy, however, is that it may not always be possible to implement it. Implementation may be particularly difficult when a situation is becoming hostile and adversarial, but is not yet overtly so, and when one party has an official reason, for supervisory or other purposes, to meet with the other party.

Tell friends about the wrongdoing. The advantage is that friends can provide support and later substantiate your version of events. The disadvantage is that you may give friends an overdose of your problems and "wear them out."

By all means, keep friends informed of what is going on. If you do not, you will become isolated and depressed, and you will make less solid judgments. Friends can provide important emotional support. Telling friends also has the advantage that they can later substantiate your version of the story. Although they may not be direct witnesses to coming events, they can substantiate timing, your concerns, and your discussions of your intentions and motives. One problem with this strategy is that if you lean too heavily on friends, you may exhaust them as well as yourself.

Go up the chain of command pursuing relief. The advantage is that you are using the formal university hierarchy in the least threatening manner. The disadvantage is that weak leadership at the top may create a lack of will up and down the chain of command for dealing with tough ethical dilemmas.

If you are unjustly accused of unethical behavior, you may go up the chain of command, seeking a redress. By staying within official channels, you will be more likely to be viewed as a team player and someone who respects system norms.

This strategy, however, is only as good as the courage and ethics of people in the chain of command.

Learn about the grievance process in case you need it. Because you must exhaust internal grievance procedures before turning to the courts, learning about these procedures ahead of time is an advantage. Grievance committees may consist wholly or partially of faculty members, which may work to your advantage. The disadvantage is that grievance boards and appeals panels may play university politics.

Find out about the grievance process in your university before you need it. In some settings, only a small "window of opportunity" is provided for filing an official grievance, sometimes as short as 30 or 45 days. Grievances and appeals not filed within that window are considered illegitimate and are not accepted. Also, failing to use internal remedies first may preclude court remedies.

Be cautious in informal written communications such as E-mail as well as formal written memos, because both can be subpoenaed in court. The advantage is that E-mail is often more spontaneous than other forms of communication. The disadvantage is that E-mail and other memos may be used out of context to undermine your case.

In many modern organizations including most universities, electronic mail has become an indispensable form of communication supplementing, if not supplanting, more traditional forms. E-mail is often more spontaneous than other forms. Telephone tag is virtually eliminated. Further, communications can occur and be received at all hours of the day and night. Night owls may type away into the wee hours of the morning, knowing their messages will be retrieved by early-morning colleagues. However, be cautious with E-mail, because tapes of E-mail messages have been subpoenaed in court cases emerging from some grievance cases that were not successfully resolved internally. Nor is the confidentiality of

E-mail ever assured, as system workers and hackers can break into your private E-mail message box. Further, E-mail messages may be used out of context to undermine your case.

Threaten a lawsuit. The advantage is that it is cheaper than actually suing. The disadvantage is that you may have to sue, and a threat must be backed up to have force.

You too, like many accused before you, can threaten a lawsuit against the accuser. Sometimes the mere threat can have a chilling effect on the behavior of others, and a threat is cheaper than an actual lawsuit. Ultimately, however, a threat may be insufficient. You may find you have to back up the threat with the expense, time, and energy of an actual lawsuit.

PART III

How to Stop Ethical Violations

7 | Choosing a Strategy for Coping With Unethical Colleagues

W hy will you, an upstanding, ethical academician, need a repertoire of strategies to cope with unethical behavior by colleagues? The extent of unethical behavior is not known. No systematic data exist documenting how broad the problem is. Definitions of ethics and standards for academic conduct may vary. Much unethical behavior goes undetected, and even when university officials are cognizant of wrongdoing, they may be anxious to keep it hidden from general and public view. Other than the AAUP, which censures colleges and schools for tenure violations, no central organization keeps track of the incidence of ethics violations. Anecdotal evidence, however, indicates that ethics violations are pervasive. No sector of the academy is immune.

Perhaps you will be lucky to find a setting where breach of ethical norms is negligible or nonexistent. But more likely, sometime in your career you will encounter wrongdoing so distressing you agonize over what to do about it. So what should you do when you encounter unethical behavior by colleagues? Should you do as Mike and Richard did in Chapter 1 and file formal charges requesting an official investigation? Should you do as their dean wanted and ignore it?

Table 7.1 Strategies for Coping With Wrongdoing by Others

	Informal	Formal
Internal	Individual strategies	Administrative and grievance strategies
External	Peer and media strategies	Professional association, court, and legislative strategies

Reputations and careers—including yours—hang on the option you choose.

There is no happy solution to unethical behavior. Rather, you may decide what to do from a range of options or strategies. Your choice is like picking your way through a minefield, trying to get to the other side and avoiding being blown up. The strategy you pick will depend, in part, on how powerful you are within the university. If you are a high-level administrator, your power is greater than if you are a department chair. Senior tenured faculty have greater power to withstand the backlash of bringing ethical violations to public scrutiny than do junior untenured faculty.

We have divided the strategies from which you might select into four categories (see Table 7.1). Strategies may be *internal* or *external* to your college. A young professor with few contacts in other universities and in the profession may have fewer opportunities to select an external strategy. Internal strategies are available to everyone, but some have higher costs in terms of confrontation and possible repercussions than others.

Strategies may also be *informal* or *formal*. On the surface, informal strategies seem less dangerous than formal strategies. However, surface appearances may be misleading. Whistle-blowing—going to the media and others outside of the university to broaden awareness of the problem—is an informal strategy because there are no set procedures or rules for how to do this. Whistle-blowing is also the most risky strategy you can use.

Internal Informal Options:
Individual Strategies

There are several possible individual strategies for dealing with a person engaging in unethical behavior, ranging from doing nothing to confronting the violator and demanding urging change. Each strategy has strengths and weaknesses.

Ignore the ethical dilemma. The advantage is that you can maintain normal, uninterrupted relationships with your colleagues. The disadvantage is that the ethical breach goes uncorrected and may continue.

The path of least resistance is to ignore the problem and the person who is creating it. This may be the safest strategy. The greater the power differential between yourself and the unethical perpetrator, the greater the risk of intervening and the more attractive doing nothing becomes. If you are junior and untenured, it may be the only strategy you feel you can use. Ignoring the dilemma may allow you to maintain normal, uninterrupted relationships with your colleagues, including the perpetrator. However, the ethical breach may go uncorrected and may continue. Evil triumphs when good people do nothing.

Discuss the dilemma in neutral terms with the perpetrator, noting similar ill-fated examples of others. The advantage is that this is the least threatening intervention. The disadvantage is that, if you do not take a strong stand, the perpetrator may view you as a co-conspirator.

Discussing the problem with the person who is creating it escalates the ante somewhat. You can point out that you are aware of the problem and find out what motivated the perpetrator to pursue an unethical course. Did he or she feel greatly pressured? If so, by whom? Are these perceptions accurate? Perhaps your insight will help the perpetrator to see that he has mentally magnified the reasons for or pressures contributing to his unethical actions, and the costs have been mentally reduced. You may talk about similar ill-fated examples. If you choose this strategy, you are acting similarly to a counselor or a psychologist, providing a mirror for feedback and a reality check, but without being strongly judgmental. This strategy has the advantage of being the least threatening type of intervention you can undertake. One disadvantage, however, is that the perpetrator may view you as a co-conspirator if you do not take a stand.

Further, your previous relationship with the perpetrator may dictate whether or not this strategy is available. If you know the perpetrator only distantly or remotely, or if you are of much lower rank and status than he or she is, you may not have the opportunity to drop by for a "chat" on the state of the world, including the perpetrator's unethical behavior. Also, the perpetrator would not likely confide in you and use you as a reality check. If, however, the perpetrator is a department colleague or someone else with whom you interact frequently and regularly, this option may be a reasonable one.

Your decision to use this strategy may rest, in part, on your assessment of the character of the perpetrator. Is the unethical action something that seems out of character and aberrant for the person committing it, possibly due to a radical change in circumstances? If so, this strategy may work. If, however, the person has previously engaged in actions consistent with the newly observed unethical action, this strategy may be less successful.

Directly confront the ethical violator and urge change. The advantage is that your concern and disapproval are clear. The disadvantage is that the violator may feel threatened and professional relations may be irreparably damaged.

With this option, you directly confront the persons engaging in unethical behavior and urge or even demand that they change. This is a risky strategy. Direct confrontation raises the possibility of a heated and hostile exchange. Your prior relationship with the accused may also influence how the perpetrator reacts. If you were once close, the perpetrator may view you as betraying him, and the potential for fractured feelings and an angry reaction increases. If you hardly knew the perpetrator beforehand, the element of personal betrayal is less strong. But the perpetrator may also more easily dismiss your concerns. If the perpetrator ignores you, you now have the worst of situations: You have changed nothing, but you have likely damaged your relationship with colleagues and possibly evoked retaliation.

Where and how do you engage in such a confrontation? If you do so in private, the ethical violator can later deny that the occasion ever occurred or interpret it to himself and others so as to reflect badly on you. If you evoke the exchange in front of others, however, the perpetrator may become very angry and seek revenge. The broader the audience before which such an exchange occurs, the greater is the likelihood of retaliation by the perpetrator. Direct confrontation in front of one or two other colleagues who regularly go to lunch together is less threatening than a confrontation in front of the entire department. One word of warning here: If you feel very upset about the unethical behavior, you may inadvertently confront the perpetrator under less-than-ideal circumstances, when you are disputing some other issue. If you choose direct confrontation as a strategy, it is best to plan beforehand when to have the confrontation and what to say, and then to follow through as calmly and unemotionally as possible.

Internal Formal Options:
Administrative and Grievance Strategies

What do you do if your attempts to resolve the ethical dilemma individually fail? Perhaps, like Mike and Richard in Chapter 1, you will find that previous departmental fighting and collegial interactions have destroyed all trust and all hope of dealing with the problem on an informal basis. Internally, several formal options are available. Formal options are generally far more serious than informal ones, and the stakes for your career escalate.

Write a memo requiring a formal response about the ethical issue to your department chair. The advantage is that this alerts the person responsible for managing the department of the problem. The disadvantage is that the department chair may inform the accused of how he or she became aware of the problem.

The decision to put your complaint into writing is a big one. You have now moved from the realm of casual observer in what could be interpreted as a collegial atmosphere to an adversarial one more closely approximating a formal plaintiff in a quasi-judicial procedure. Unlike in the courts, however, the process for administrative remedies may be less clearly defined. Unlike Freedom of Information Act requests for information from the government, which require a response within a specified number of days, within universities no formal requirements may exist about time frames for responses to ethical dilemmas.

You increase the likelihood of a timely response if you "cc" or send a courtesy copy to the dean and to higher administrative officials. When you copy a memo, the convention is to list at the bottom, beside the abbreviation "cc", the names of the additional persons to whom the memo is being sent. This alerts higher officials to a brewing problem and may put pressure on the department chair to act promptly. But it may make your department chair angry as well as the person you are accusing of unethical behavior. The chair may interpret the "cc" as a veiled threat to dispose of the matter in the fashion you request or you will file formal charges. The chair may worry about how he or she looks to higher administrative officials and may get angry at you for making it look as if he or she cannot manage the department well.

The strategy of a formal memo to your chair has the advantage of making the person with direct responsibility for managing the department aware of the ethical problem. One disadvantage is that the chair may inform the accused of your actions, using unfavorable terms. You may be portrayed as the "fall guy" or "heavy" for calling attention to the unethical behavior, whereas the chair becomes the "rescuer" attempting to fix the problem.

Send direct memos about the ethical dilemma beyond the department chair up the chain of command. The advantage is that you are demanding a response from those with the greatest clout in the university. The disadvantage is that, if you send too many memos to higher officials or send ones dealing with petty issues, you will be ignored or viewed as a troublemaker.

If your department chair is unresponsive to an ethical problem, you may send memos directly to the dean and higher officials up the chain of command, including the provost and the president. Unlike "cc'ed" memos that higher officials can ignore, this strategy forces them to deal with the ethical dilemma directly. The risk of alienating your chair with this strategy is even greater, however. Clever and cautious higher officials may still duck the issue by writing a response that shows sympathy with your viewpoint but does not promise resolution, or by just acknowledging your memo without showing any sympathy. If you pursue this option too frequently, you will be regarded as a troublemaker who spends more time trying to run the university than doing your own job.

Not everyone up the chain of command may be equally sympathetic or willing to address the unethical behavior to which you have pointed. By jumping the chain of command and going to higher level officials while skipping over one or more lower level ones, you can get around "roadblocks" in addressing the problem. However, those jumped over may become resentful when they discover what you have done and they may try to sabotage your request for action. You also run the risk that the higher officials you approach may kick the problem right back to the people you jumped over, arguing that administrative procedures and hierarchy should not be violated.

Submit a charge to a grievance or appeals body. The advantage is that such bodies usually include faculty who may be more sensitive to your concerns. The disadvantage is that, in an administrative setting, this is the equivalent to a formal declaration of war.

Is the unethical colleague who is causing you concern also causing you personal harm or professional damage? If so, you can submit a formal charge to a grievance or appeals body within the university. Your filing will result in a hearing on the issue and will force some resolution. Grievance and appeals bodies usually include faculty, who may be more sensitive to your concerns than administrative officials, who are focused on budgets, programs, and other aspects of operations.

In an administrative setting, filing a formal charge or grievance is the organizational equivalent to a formal declaration of war. If you do not file, as, in a somewhat different setting Anita Hill declined to file formal sexual harassment charges against Clarence Thomas, former director of the EEOC, your action may later be interpreted as confirming that no problem existed. If you do file, however, expect the full wrath of the accused and any powerful friends he or she may have to fall on your head.

External Informal Options:
Peer and Media Strategies

Your options for dealing with ethical dilemmas are not restricted to those internal to your college or university. If the climate inside your university is unfavorable toward your cause, you may pursue external remedies. One strategy that people "losing" in one setting have pursued is to broaden the arena of conflict. For example, rebels in a civil war losing on strictly military terms may broaden the conflict through guerilla warfare to include the civilian population. Pursuing external remedies to resolve an ethical dilemma is a similar approach. Although informal peer interactions with colleagues at other universities may be less serious than pursuing formal options internal to your university, make no mistake about the seriousness of going to the media. If you go to the media with ethical wrongdoing, you are not only pursuing the same strategy employed by rebels in guerilla warfare: You have become one.

Discuss the unethical behavior at your own college with peers at other universities to gain their input and support. The advantage is that this allows you to get advice and input from colleagues with a different institutional perspective. The disadvantage is that this does little to address the immediate case at hand and you may be viewed as a rumormonger.

When you first become aware of an ethical problem, you may have never confronted such a situation. You may be disturbed and uneasy but not able to fully articulate why. Or you may know that wrongdoing is going on but wonder if you are blowing things out of proportion. At this point, discussions with colleagues at other universities about the problem may provide input from people with different institutional perspectives. They can provide a reality check to confirm if you are interpreting the ethical dilemma in a reasonable manner. If you temper your discussion and use discretion, you may not be perceived as impugning the character of colleagues or be perceived as a gossiper.

The disadvantage of this strategy, however, is that other than informing your judgment this option does little to address the immediate matter at hand. The reaction by outside colleagues to your revelations may depend, in part, on how frequently and in what context you discuss the ethical breach that concerns you. If you discuss it initially at the time it first occurs or at the time you first become aware of it, expressing genuine concern over the implications of the dilemma being unresolved, your image as a helpful colleague may remain intact. If the situation is ongoing and never-ending, and your discussions of it also seem endless, you may wear out friends and other peers outside your institution. They may grow weary of hearing you talk about the dilemma, and you may be perceived as a possessed zealot. Further, word may get back to the ethics violator that you are "sandbagging" them by spreading rumors that you have not officially substantiated. The battle becomes one of credibility and a question of whose is greater: yours, the accuser, or that of the accused ethical violator.

Your discussions of the dilemma externally may not correct the immediate problem, but you may ultimately do harm to the perpetrator. If you are a senior faculty member or one to whom others might turn for advice or recommendations, you can convey the dilemma and your concern over it when your opinion is being sought. Often when a colleague has applied elsewhere for a position at another university, faculty at the department where the job application is being made will informally call up friends at the applicant's department to get the "real scoop" on the applicant. If you find yourself in this situation, you may be torn. If you reveal the unethical behavior, the friends may convey it to the search committee who will likely kill the chances of your unethically behaving colleague getting the job. On the one hand, you have inhibited the colleague's chances of advancement and justifiably revealed his true behavior. On the other hand, you may be stuck with the unethical colleague as a department member for the indefinite future. However, if you do not reveal information about the unethical behavior when asked to give a true opinion in an informal setting that would not redound immediately to your detriment, you may suffer repercussions. If the unethical colleague is hired elsewhere and continues his unethical practices, friends who turned to you for advice may become angry at you for passing off your "problem" onto them.

Further, the strategy of conveying to others outside the university what has happened to the detriment of the perpetrator only works if the perpetrator has any dealings of importance with external colleagues. If the perpetrator has no interest in applying for a job elsewhere, rarely goes to professional meetings or makes presentations, and does not publish or apply for grants, he may interact little or not at all with peers elsewhere. The perpetrator may want and expect nothing from them, content to stay in a safe tenured position at your current university, oblivious to the larger professional community.

Try to interest campus publications in the unethical behavior. The advantage is that administrators may subsequently experience broad campuswide pressure to resolve the ethical dilemma. The disadvantage is that you may be cast as a muckraker and need to worry about libel and slander countercharges if your charge is not well substantiated.

If administrative officials in your university are ignoring the unethical behavior, or if you feel going to them is too risky, you may try to interest campus publications in the dilemma. Young student journalists may view themselves as the equivalent of Woodward and Bernstein, whose investigative reporting contributed to the demise of President Richard Nixon over Watergate. You may use their desires to muckrake and bring down powerful figures to stimulate an investigation into the wrongdoing that concerns you.

If this strategy is successful, administrators may subsequently experience broad campuswide pressure to resolve the ethical dilemma. Yet many factors may thwart a successful outcome. First, you must decide whether to be the campus equivalent of "Deep Throat," retaining anonymity, or to make the accusations publicly and be quoted in the campus publication. If you decide to go the Deep Throat route, you have no assurances that student reporters will not inadvertently or under pressure from authorities reveal your identity. If your identity is made known in this fashion, the anger the perpetrator subsequently directs toward you could be even greater than if you had made the charges up front in some other forum. If you eschew the cloak and dagger of Deep Throat and make public charges with quotes for the paper, you of course set yourself up for a public counterattack.

Not all cases of unethical behavior by professors or administrators are amenable to student investigations. Students may not have the authority or capacity to adequately investigate some types of charges, such as unethical behavior in research or faculty stealing credit for work from others. You may find that the quality of student reporting varies widely, with some reporters reporting in a reasonable and accurate manner and others not capturing the essence of the story. Fighting things out in student newspapers may not be the effective way to address unethical wrongdoing. At some point, however, you may feel that you have few other options.

Try to interest the general media in the wrongdoing. The advantage is that this extends concern to the public. The disadvantage is that only a limited number of academic issues will be of interest to the broader public.

Broadening the conflict to the general public escalates the stakes immensely. Even if you are successful, this is one of the forms of whistle-blowing that in other types of organizations could cause you lose status or even be terminated. In recent years, as the economy has tightened, state budgets have grown more lean, tuitions at both public and private institutions have escalated, and the general public attitude toward higher education has grown more hostile. Books such as *Profscam* (Sykes, 1988) and *The Closing of the American Mind* (Bloom, 1987) have cast professors and universities in a bad light. Academic institutions are viewed as administratively bloated and fat. Faculty governance is presented as clumsy, conflictual, and glacial. Professors are presented as autonomous and independent, caring little about the institution or the quality of teaching, despite low teaching loads compared to junior colleges and secondary education. Tenured faculty are viewed both as benefiting from job security greater than in any other sector in the workforce and as flaunting the lack of accountability that such security brings.

Calling attention in the general media to unethical behavior within the university in such a public climate will definitely gain the attention of university administrators. Depending on the extent of the coverage, some reaction from the university officials will likely be forthcoming. You, however, may be subjected to threatened or actual lawsuits for slander or libel if your charge is not well substantiated. Your job mobility may plummet as prospective employers become fearful that you are a disgruntled publicity seeker. Further, the media have no power to directly force a certain administrative ruling or to enforce justice in any particular institutional setting. Unless media coverage results in pressure within the university or governing body to do so, your pain may be for naught. (See James Alan Fox and Jack Levin's [1993] book *How to Work With the Media* in this series for help on that topic.)

External Formal Options: Professional Association, Court, and Legislative Strategies

A fourth set of options for dealing with the unethical behavior of others involves formal remedies external to the university. These are very serious strategies with great potential and great risk. Along with the informal external strategy of going to the media, these are the most serious strategies you can pursue. In most instances, they involve public exposure, time, and effort. Some also involve financial costs.

Discuss the dilemma with outside accreditors and disciplinary program reviewers. The advantage is that outside accreditors may consider the ethical issues when writing up their reports. The disadvantage is that you may be seen as trying to sabotage the accreditation over what some university personnel feel is a tangential issue.

Some ethical violations are of sufficient magnitude that they impact on the quality of academic programs and on the quality of services rendered to students. Universities must undergo some type of accreditation, often by regional accrediting bodies. In some instances, specific disciplinary accreditation is also required, as in the case of engineering, business administration, public administration, and many other fields. Even when disciplinary accreditation is not necessary, the board of trustees or the state commission on higher education may request that a team of outside reviewers come in and examine the functioning of a department.

Elaborate self-studies and data collection precede the actual on-campus visit by a team of accreditors. The purpose of the accreditors is to look at general program issues rather than specific cases and grievances, but unethical behavior that impacts program integrity is of interest to the visiting team. If you choose to talk with the outside reviewers and discuss the troubling unethical behavior, the team may include your concerns in their deliberations and reports. In turn, this may lead to the correction of processes that allowed the unethical behavior to persist.

There are several disadvantages to this strategy, however. First, accreditation visits are intermittent, occurring at intervals of 5 to 10 years unless major problems have been encountered on the previous accreditation visit. Thus an accreditation visit several years into the future will not address immediate wrongdoing. Second, even if an accreditation visit is imminent, the process of writing the report and having the findings reported to appropriate university officials may take months. Again, immediate relief is not forthcoming. Third, as mentioned, accreditors cannot become embroiled in the details of any particular case, unless it threatens the functioning of the program or university. Finally, if your actions are found out by your colleagues or by university administrators, you may be seen as trying to sabotage the accreditation over what some university personnel may feel is a personal or tangential issue.

Lodge a formal charge with an ethics committee of your professional association. The advantage is that this may bring disciplinewide attention to your university neglecting to deal with the problem. The disadvantage is that professional ethics committees have few or no formal sanctions and are left mostly with moral suasion.

Most professional associations have formal ethics committees as part of their standing committee structure. These committees are charged with developing ethics codes for the association and its members. But often, these professional ethics committees will also hold hearings and render rulings concerning particular ethics violations at specific institutions. The committees then publicize their results in professional journals and publications. By doing so, the committees may indirectly exert pressure on the institution in which wrongdoing has been perpetrated to address the problem. This strategy has the advantage of bringing professionwide attention to the ethics violation of concern. One disadvantage, however, is that external professional ethics committees often have no jurisdiction over decisions in any specific university or college. Thus they may have limited ability to engage in a full-fledged investigation if the accused is uncooperative. They also have no formal authority within the institution to enforce any remedy. Their primary power remains that of professional and peer opinion and moral suasion.

After exhausting internal remedies, get a lawyer and sue. The advantage is that the courts may be more favorable and their decisions are binding. The disadvantage is that legal action can be very expensive in money, time, and energy.

In some settings, when all other remedies are either not available or have failed, and when you have been personally affected or even the object of the unethical behavior, you may have no other recourse than the common American cure to many ills: a lawsuit. If university administrators have been ignoring your concerns previously, they will definitely pay attention when they are named as defendants in a civil lawsuit. The courts may provide the relief you have been denied elsewhere. The disadvantage of a lawsuit, however, is the high cost. Lawyers who understand academic issues are neither prolific nor cheap. Further, the lawsuit may take an emotional toll and distract you from productive, career-enhancing endeavors.

Try to evoke a legislative investigation. The advantage is that university administrators pay attention to legislators who hold "the power of the purse." The disadvantage is that legislators are very busy and may not be interested in issues not well understood by the public.

One strategy available at state universities and colleges is to try to evoke a legislative investigation. You may do this by calling your own representative or senator or a member of the legislature who is particularly sensitive to higher education issues. The advantage of this option is that university administrators care deeply about the opinions and concerns of politicians who hold the power of the purse. A disadvantage is that once the issue is tossed into the volatile, free-for-all political arena, you may lose control of it and may see ramifications you did not anticipate. The politician may try to use the unethical behavior to gain personal publicity for his or her reelection campaign as a defender of the public trust. Further, legislators are very busy, and some may not be interested in issues that are unfamiliar to the public. This strategy may also backfire if the controversy and scandal become ammunition for proponents of future funding cuts. Of course, faculty at private universities have little reason to involve state politicians or state authorities, unless the issue is so grave as to influence state accreditation or approval. Going to the board of trustees, who are quasi-external but also theoretically in the internal chain of command, is a strategy similar in character, which may be used by faculty at both public and private institutions.

Choosing Wisely

If events heat up and begin to transpire rapidly, you may not consciously pick a strategy for dealing with the ethical dilemma but just try whatever occurs to you at the time. Doing so, however, is ill-advised, as each strategy has strengths and weaknesses as discussed above. It is better to think through your situation, including your role and position within the university, with a critical eye on your real capacity to bring about change. Being naive initially will not offset the pain you may experience subsequently if you do not choose wisely. Think through the consequences with a best and worst scenario for each strategy under consideration. If the worst scenario has consequences that you do not wish to incur, then eliminate that strategy and select another one. The career at stake may be your own.

8 | When Informal Strategies Do Not Work

Sometimes informal strategies do not work for resolving ethical dilemmas. You may find yourself swept into a grievance procedure and legal action. At this point, your struggles to behave ethically have become adversarial. In the case of an internal grievance, you are an adversary with your very employer, the college or the university where you work. Through a grievance process, you are trying to get the university to correct a wrongdoing that has not been adequately addressed. The wrongdoing may involve a particular colleague or administrator or may be more generalized to the broader university administrative structure.

If the grievance process is unsuccessful, you may continue the battle into court. In universities with a strong faculty union and a collective bargaining process, the grievance process is negotiated as part of the collective bargaining agreement. Consultation with your AAUP representative about grievance procedures is appropriate.

We are grateful to the University of Michigan Press for permission to adapt and paraphrase material from *Academics in Court* (1987), by George LaNoue and Barbara Lee. Also, material from Joseph Becker's *Faculty Staff Nonrenewal and Dismissal for Cause in Institutions of High Education* (1986) has been adapted with permission of the publisher, College Administration Publications, Inc., Asheville, NC.

Faculty involved in grievance procedures sometimes do not hire a lawyer at the outset of any dispute unless they have every intention of filing a civil lawsuit. Even at this stage, however, the stakes of winning and losing are escalating and consulting with a lawyer may keep you from making key errors. Some AAUP chapters may provide limited legal assistance or advice on where to find a lawyer who is familiar with academic affairs and faculty issues.

Using Formal Remedies to Save a Career

Consider the case of Joyce, who taught at a midsize university. On the surface, Joyce seemed outgoing, enthusiastic about her work, friendly, plucky, and interesting. Closer inspection, however, revealed that Joyce was regarded by her department colleagues as a walking time bomb, and they kept their distance.

Joyce had come to the university as an untenured assistant professor. After her marriage she had returned to graduate school to complete her doctorate. Both her department, and the whole university were developing higher standards of publishing. When Joyce arrived, numerous department colleagues published little or nothing. By contrast, Joyce had published regularly, including a couple of articles a year and two books prior to her tenure decision.

Joyce's department was headed by an autocrat, Phil, who exuded elitist attitudes but published little himself. He had cultivated personal loyalty among department members and had created a "lunch bunch" of supportive colleagues. Every day, the group would march en masse to lunch, dining in various restaurants around the campus, making a big show of who was included versus who was excluded. Joyce was never in the department chair's lunch bunch. Because Phil was such a strong personality, generally recruited people who would not challenge his leadership, and kept a firm grip on department resources, he remained chair for a long time.

The evolving standards of the university and Phil's leadership coincided with a period of growing student demand for his department's courses and for a while made it seem to an outside observer that Phil was doing a good job as department chair. But inside the department, trouble was brewing, particularly between Phil and Joyce. The two developed a strong dislike for each other. Joyce, no shrinking violet, did not follow Phil appreciatively nor did she dote on his lunch jokes and clever mind. Phil viewed Joyce as not only difficult but weird. Unlike other department members who invested much emotional energy into department relations, Joyce did not, having her emotional roots in groups outside of the university, especially her religion. On any given occasion, Joyce could break into conversation about the need to commune with spirits, nature, inner self, and a whole host of other phenomena that baffled, puzzled, and bewildered her department colleagues. Nonetheless, Joyce also taught her subject well and was a reasonably popular teacher. The number of her publications exceeded that of most department members.

Privately, Joyce would reveal that Phil, a married man, had "come on" to her sexually not long after she arrived. She would discuss a sequence of events that started out innocently enough, from Phil dropping by her office to inquire about her work to calling her in for private conferences in his office where the conversation would move from professional matters to personal matters and then to intimate issues. Eventually, his actions escalated to calling her at home and finally trying to set up private work sessions under conditions that would lead to sex. Perhaps Joyce was flattered initially by the special attention, given the sycophancy of the lunch bunch, each clamoring to gain Phil's good graces. As his actions became more and more sexual in context and content, she became more and more alarmed. She did not want an affair with someone who had so much power over her life, and eventually, she plainly and unequivocally rebuffed Phil's advances. As an untenured assistant professor in a chair-dominated department, and because policies against sexual harassment were at that point embryonic, Joyce did not file charges of sexual harassment against Phil. She feared he would be revengeful and knew she would have difficulty proving her case. She knew that Phil, not a particularly handsome man himself, would try to twist her charges to make it look as if she were a lonely, large, sex-starved, divorced woman coming on to him. After all, she had initially been flattered by the extra attention until it became so explicitly sexual and quid pro quo in character. He would imply that he was a happily married man and that she was so unappealing that the idea of him making advances was ludicrous. Furthermore, he could rely on the testimony of the lunch bunch for corroboration.

Joyce decided to try to tough it out through tenure by working so hard and producing so much that the department could not possibly turn her down.

Later, Joyce wondered if she had made a mistake, because then the harassment began. Phil stripped Joyce of perks, travel money, and resources. She was assigned to teach a series of 8:00 a.m. classes on the same days she also had to teach at night. Her teaching load, despite her research productivity, was heavy, the maximum allowed. Her classes were large and had no teaching assistants. As Phil became more and more critical of her, other department colleagues who depended on him for rewards also became more distant, excluding her from informal social activities or communication.

During the next few years, Joyce relied heavily on the grievance and legal processes. Otherwise she would have been driven away from the university and her job. She tried to appeal to the dean on small issues, but by now, she was viewed as a troublemaker, a large, assertive woman with unconventional views. The dean chose to ignore Joyce's complaints. He would not pursue a course of action without majority faculty support. Phil's department, however, was run autocratically with Phil able to control majority opinion.

When Joyce came up for tenure, Phil opposed it and was able to marshal a majority vote within the department against her. Joyce was stunned, having hoped that her record would be evaluated on its merits and that department politics would be laid aside. Consistent with his previous stance, the dean refused to challenge the department chair and the majority vote. He supported the department's decision.

The schoolwide tenure and promotion committee chose to interpret its role very narrowly by not ruling on the merits of any tenure case, but by examining the process for procedural violations. There had been none. Thus the school committee voted to decline tenure. When the file reached the provost, it had three preceding "no's" attached to it. The provost declined to overturn the decisions made at lower levels. The president, almost ready to retire and never much involved in internal affairs, followed the lead of his provost.

Having few close friends in the department or school, Joyce called a lawyer specializing in issues related to higher education who encouraged her to file a grievance. Her case was forwarded to a special grievance committee whose function was to deal with tenure and promotion appeals. She did little additional preparation, other than to submit an appeals memo, stating that she disagreed with the decision to deny her tenure, and recapping her academic record and how it met prevailing department standards. In the memo, she also compared her record to that of men in the department who had recently been awarded tenure. The appeals committee of administrators and senior faculty members from various departments judged that Joyce's record did meet the prevailing standards for tenure in her department and the university.

Joyce won her appeal and was granted tenure, but the harassment did not stop. Two more times she turned to formal remedies. One instance involved her teaching. Joyce taught courses that dealt with sexual violence and sexual offenders, reporting studies of background correlates, psychological profiles, incidence, effectiveness of public policies, and correctional actions. Some of the studies and relevant court cases used sexually explicit words. Phil, angry at Joyce being granted tenure on appeal, encouraged the students to complain about her classroom language and discussion of sexually explicit events. Of course, she had taught these courses for several years, trying to keep them updated and current as the case law and research concerning sexual offenses was continuously changing. A big conflict emerged and Phil threatened to penalize Joyce on annual reviews because of these "complaints." Joyce threatened to file a grievance and to get a lawyer and sue. In this instance, she had standardized teaching evaluations to back up her claim that she was a competent teacher. Phil asserted that the overall evaluations did not deal with this particular problem, but nevertheless he backed down.

Eventually, however, Joyce did get a lawyer and sued for sexual discrimination when she found out that she was making several thousand dollars less than men in the department of equal or lower rank who had published much less. First she approached the dean and the provost, but they argued that there was no money available for salary adjustments. Then Joyce sued. The trial was delayed several times. Before her case came to trial, the university had a transition in leadership. Joyce was offered a partial settlement for back pay differentials, plus a salary equal to that of the less productive men at her rank. Fatigued from all the conflict and legal clashes, Joyce accepted the settlement offer. Had university grievance processes and legal actions not been available to her, her career would likely have ended at tenure. Had she not been willing to use the procedures when she felt that others, especially Phil, were acting unethically, she would not have survived professionally.

What Should You Know
About Using the Grievance Process?

If you wish to use the grievance process at your university, what should you know to do so? The example of Joyce points to several issues and tips to consider if you are thinking of filing a formal grievance.

Be familiar with the grievance process in your particular university. Not all universities have elaborate grievance processes with clearly specified procedures. Procedures may vary from university to university. If you find yourself entrapped in a growing ethical dilemma and suspect that there is any possibility you may at some point file a formal grievance, find the grievance procedures. You may not wish to alert your department chair and colleagues about your intentions by asking them where the grievance procedures can be located. Check the faculty handbook as a possible location. In some universities, though, grievance procedures may be in a separate pamphlet or publication. The university personnel administrator should be able to direct you to the appropriate location. You may also check with the president of the faculty senate, and in some instances, the EEOC officer.

Universities with active AAUP units that negotiate regular collective bargaining contracts affecting faculty raises and working conditions are more likely to have well-specified procedures. In universities and small colleges that are not unionized, grievance procedures may be limited in scope and vague, as they were at Midstate University in the beginning chapter. Yet most universities and colleges have some form of grievance procedure, specified either in the faculty handbook or in a separate document. Find it and read it thoroughly to ascertain if your case is covered, what documentation is needed, and how to proceed.

Grievance proceedings are often more elaborate and clear for denial of tenure or job termination than for other forms of wrongdoing. Universities and colleges are most likely to have grievance procedures that cover major actions affecting job status and continuation of employment. General administrative procedures may not directly cover other ethical issues, such as discrimination in assignment of classes and department support, spreading false rumors, and fraud in research. Some universities may have grievance procedures clearly suitable to these other areas, but others, particularly in nonunionized settings and smaller colleges, may have only vague procedures or none at all. The procedures for grieving a wrong perpetrated against you are also usually more clearly specified than those for filing formal charges concerning the wrongdoing of others, unless their actions impact personally and negatively on you.

Timeliness in meeting deadlines is crucial. Numerous deadlines exist in most grievance processes that pertain to job termination and tenure. The most crucial is the initial deadline for filing the grievance itself. In unionized settings, grieving faculty often have two important deadlines: first to file an intent to grieve, and second, to file the actual grievance statement. Failure to do this in a timely fashion precludes you from using the grievance process as a remedy.

The grievance process can be lengthy. The grievance process can be long, taking months, not days, and even consuming the better part of a year, if each stage reaches the maximum allowable duration before being forwarded to the next phase. This is quite lengthy. During this interim when no decision has yet been rendered, you may be forced to work in an uncomfortable and even hostile environment. There is little you can do to shorten the process, other than mentally be prepared when filing a grievance for a relatively long siege.

The process is quasi-judicial and adversarial. Although formal courtroom rules of evidence do not strictly apply, the grievance process is quasi-judicial and adversarial. Just as legal charges must be classified and linked to particular laws, grievance allegations must be filed in particular categories and linked to violations of specific collective bargaining agreements or university policies and procedures. When filing a grievance, you become an adversary, first, of the individuals or group whom you charge with the wrongdoing or bias, and second, of the university, which sustained their behavior and decisions until your grievance called them into question. Do not underestimate the fact that deans and other university administrators may view your grievance as an indirect charge against their competence and judgment, as well as against those whom you name formally in your grievance as the source of the immediate harm.

If your faculty is unionized, check with your AAUP office for advice and support in making your grievance. Some campuses have an active chapter of the AAUP, which can provide invaluable advice and support to you throughout the grievance process. Make sure you check with your AAUP representative when you are considering filing an appeal. The representative will help you assess whether or not your grievance fits into an allowable category, assess the likelihood of winning, and organize the facts and witnesses surrounding your case.

Make only allegations you can substantiate. When making formal charges, make only ones you can document and substantiate. You will be helped in your documentation if, at this point, you have kept a file of memos, letters, reports, and other information on the growing confrontation. If you make unsubstantiated charges, you are opening yourself up to countercharges of being unprofessional and even slanderous and libelous. Further, in strained situations, one round of unsubstantiated charges may be met by a return volley of the same until the situation escalates out of control. Remember that in filing a grievance, the burden of proof is on you.

Know and identify the remedy you want. If your grievance concerns unethical wrongdoing perpetrated against you, know what you want done to correct the situation. If your job has been jeopardized by denial of tenure or failure to have an employment contract renewed, the immediately obvious remedy is the restoration of your job. Depending on the situation, however, other remedies may also be appropriate, including awarding back pay, remedying salary differentials, reallocating class assignments, and, in harassment cases, an administrative equivalent of a court restraining order directing the perpetrator to cease and desist the harassment and setting up a monitoring procedure to verify if the order is being followed. If in the process of filing the grievance, relationships have gotten so hostile in your current department as to preclude any likelihood of your being an effective faculty member and scholar in the near future, you might consider negotiating a switch to an alternate unit in the university as part of the remedy. You may even retain the right to return to your current department at some future point.

Be open to settling the issue informally at any stage of the process. Remain open to settling the dispute that prompted you to file the grievance informally if an offer to do so is made. While in the heat of conflict, you may wish to carry the grievance to its final resolution, remember your purpose is to find a remedy for a pressing ethical problem that may be impacting directly on your welfare and career. Prolonging the conflict interrupts your ability to work and may further sour relationships with department colleagues. Of course, the settlement must be a reasonable one. At some point, ending the conflict and getting on with your life may be more important than taking a chance that the final grievance report will provide you more satisfaction.

Confidentiality and discretion are important. If you are angry and upset about the situation that prompted you to file the grievance, you may feel a need to discuss the issue and its details. Do so only with close family members and friends whom you can trust not to breach your confidence. Confidentiality is often an implied part of filing a grievance, and indeed, in some cases, an overt requirement. Failure to protect confidentiality may further inflame the situation and eventually be used against you. If your lack of discretion does not become an issue in the grievance process itself, it may cause you to be viewed as not a team player, when your situation is already fragile.

If you do not file a grievance, you may be precluded from suing.
Many courts require that in issues relating to employment, discrimination, harassment, and so on a plaintiff in the legal
system have first exhausted internal remedies seeking a solution to the problem. Thus, if you do not file a grievance, you
have not exhausted internal remedies, and you may fail to
win "standing to sue," which would allow you to bring a
lawsuit against the university or some of its administrators.

Should You Sue?

If your internal grievance fails, you may wish to continue
your case through legal remedies. If you initiate the lawsuit,
of course, you are the plaintiff, and the university or some
administrators and colleagues are the defendants. If you are
named in a lawsuit brought by someone else who contends
you have violated his or her rights, you are the defendant. In
Academics in Court, LaNoue and Lee (1987, pp. 43-48) discuss
the process of academic lawsuits in detail. In deciding whether
to sue, you will confront several major issues, which are
described below.

Evaluating the Triggering Event

Many circumstances may lead to a lawsuit. Discrimination
in failure to hire; denial of tenure or promotion; and unfair
salaries, benefits, and working conditions can all be triggering events. Discrimination based on race, gender, age, religion, and ethnic origin may all be bases for lawsuits. Because
subsequent legal strategies depend on the triggering event,
its definition has important consequences. In this stage, you
must determine how you perceive the discrimination or unfair treatment versus how your legal opponents might. This
helps you decide if you have a case and anticipate and counter
their arguments for their actions. Consult with family and
friends, also, and see if they will sustain you emotionally and

perhaps even financially during the course of a prospective lawsuit.

Selecting a Lawyer

If you have decided to sue, you should select a good lawyer as early in the process as possible. Make sure in picking a lawyer that you select someone who is familiar with university processes and who knows about the unique issues surrounding tenure and discrimination within higher education. You might check with others who have filed lawsuits against the university. You might talk to your local bar association or, at universities with law schools, to faculty in the law school to get a list of names. It is important to discuss up front with a prospective lawyer his or her fees, his or her anticipation of the hours that will be involved, and his or her assessment of the probability of your winning your case.

Deciding in What Court to File

How do you decide in which court to file? Of course, your lawyer will help you make this determination. The court selected is determined by the nature of your case. If you are contending that some state law or state constitutional provision has been breached, you file in state civil court, unless a felony has been committed, such as theft or financial fraud. In this case, the district attorney decides if the case is to be prosecuted in criminal court. If, however, some federal law or constitutional right has been violated, such as the 1964 Civil Rights Act and the 1972 Equal Pay Act, you may file in federal court. Other federal grounds are violation of the Fourteenth Amendment provisions for equal rights and due process.

Preparing Your Case

You must decide the scope and framework you will use in your case. Should you seek external support, such as that of advocacy groups if it can be obtained? Does your case have sufficiently broad implications that any resolution can be applied to a larger class of potential plaintiffs and filed as a class action suit? Academic cases are often complex and involve considerable preparation, especially if they are class action suits. Preparation includes the development of a legal strategy, collection of relevant documentation, and identifying and interviewing any key witnesses. Searching for supporting precedent cases is also a part of preparation.

The pretrial period between the triggering event and the beginning of the actual trial may be quite lengthy, taking months or even years. Long periods of inactivity will be punctuated with intermittent bursts of activity, including depositions, interrogatories, motions, briefs, and pretrial hearings. Delay usually works to the advantage of the defendant, as key witnesses become cloudy in their recollections, go on sabbatical or leave, or even move to other universities. Thus it is important to have an attorney who pushes forward as quickly as possible within allowable time frames and deadlines.

Going to Trial

Reputations and careers may ride on the trial and its outcomes. The plaintiff may have to prove that he or she is a competent employee who performed well, despite charges to the contrary. If the university is the defendant, it will have to prove the soundness and legitimacy of its decision processes and that its decision makers were unbiased. All of these proofs take place under adversarial conditions with each side trying to undermine the credibility of the other side.

If you are the plaintiff suing to keep your job or to receive redress for harassment or discrimination, you will likely have more at stake in the decision than the university. The decision may determine whether or not you continue to have a job and an academic career under conditions that will allow you to be productive and to thrive. For the university, the decision may have financial consequences. If your case is a class action suit or has implications for university failure to correct some broadly seated persistent problem, the financial consequences can be considerable. Furthermore, the university may have to reform its administrative rules and decision processes as a result of a lawsuit.

Living With the Legal Outcome

Most civil suits are eventually settled out of court, because trials entail great uncertainty, unpredictability, and high costs. If a settlement is offered, consider it seriously. Sometimes partial justice is better than no justice, a determination you must make in your own case after consulting friends, family, and colleagues familiar with your case.

Even if you win your lawsuit, the fallout from the tension and costs surrounding years of litigation may be considerable. At the least, some colleagues will continue to regard you as a troublemaker who can only keep a job or deal with work issues through the court system. If your department has taken sides, it may be permanently divided in factions on this issue, and the ability to work with some colleagues may be permanently impaired. You can likely forget any aspirations of an administrative career in higher education if you ever harbored them. Even your job mobility may be restricted as knowledge of your lawsuit circulates to other schools. Administrators in other universities may nix your recruitment if they fear that your willingness to resort to a lawsuit may result in one against them.

If you lose the lawsuit, the consequences are even more devastating. You have paid tremendous financial costs for no gain, and furthermore, the other side has had its position legally vindicated. Personal costs, such as disruption of families and even divorce, may also be part of the posttrial fallout.

Deciding Whether to Appeal if You Lose

The decision to appeal to the next highest level of court is one that should carefully weigh the additional costs versus the potential gains. In federal courts, an appeal would be filed in the appropriate federal circuit court. States vary as to whether or not they have an intermediate appeals court between district court and the state supreme court, but most do.

You cannot file an appeal just because you disagree with the outcome of the district court. Rather, one of two grounds must be present. The first is a factual error or revelation of some new information bearing on the outcome of the trial that was not known at the time of the district court trial. The second is an argument that your constitutional rights have been violated. This argument may be based on violation of such rights as due process, or on the unconstitutionality of a relevant law. If your case was initially filed in a state district court, you must continue any appeal through the state court system. You cannot change to federal court, unless a question of federal constitutional rights is also involved.

Dismissing Faculty for Cause

In some lawsuits, your job may be at stake if you are the one charged with unethical behavior. Joseph Beckham (1986) provides an excellent overview of issues surrounding dismissal of faculty in *Faculty/Staff Nonrenewal and Dismissal for Cause in Institutions of Higher Education*. Following is a summary of many of his conclusions about both grounds for dismissal of faculty and grounds for defense.

Although tenure is normally considered an entitlement, it does not protect a faculty member from dismissal for cause. Even untenured provisional faculty employed under term contracts must be given adequate cause for dismissal that breaches the terms of their contract. Normal termination based on nonrenewal of your job contract requires adequate

Table 8.1 Adequate Cause for Dismissing Faculty

Incompetency
>A substantial and specific lack of ability that renders an employee unable to effectively perform teaching or other duties imposed by the university.

Neglect of duty
>Failing to meet duties related to all aspects of faculty job requirements in a timely manner.

Insubordination
>A willful disregard of reasonable directives from appropriate authorities or a defiant attitude of noncompliance toward regulations specifically applicable to a faculty.

Immoral or unethical conduct
>Varied, with no single standard, but includes conduct that offends contemporary moral standards, is inconsistent with moral rectitude, or evokes condemnation by the academic community.

---

notice of the intent to end employment of the faculty member. Employees hired for an indefinite term but not tenured are regarded as "terminable at will." Their employment can be ended without identification of adequate cause. This type of employment more frequently applies to staff than to faculty. Usual grounds for adequate cause for dismissing faculty include incompetency, neglect of duty, insubordination, and immoral or unethical conduct (see Table 8.1).

Incompetency

Incompetence occurs if there is a substantial and specific lack of ability that renders an employee unable to effectively perform teaching or other duties imposed by the university (Beckham, 1986). The employee's incompetence must be too great to remediate within a reasonable time, or the employer's attitude so recalcitrant as to be unwilling to undertake the needed remediation.

There are two steps to proving incompetence. In Step 1, the institution must identify in advance the required knowledge, skills, or competencies. In Step 2, the university must develop evaluation measures that identify and document incompetencies relative to the requirements specified in Step 1. Generally, the courts have sanctioned a wide range of university discretion in dismissing employees whose methods are judged ineffectual, whose attitudes are regarded as improper, or whose retention will directly harm students or otherwise impair the ability of the university to pursue its educational mission.

In the case of *Chung v. Park* (1975), for instance, the Third Circuit Court of Appeals upheld the dismissal of Professor Chung in his fifth year of teaching at Mansfield State College. Chung had been given previous notice of specific deficiencies, but the university contended he had made no attempt to correct the deficiencies. Chung had argued unsuccessfully that, because his notification of dismissal preceded a hearing panel on the issue, he was denied due process. The court ruled that, because his employment was continued during the hearing process, he was not denied due process. The university won.

In the case of *Jawa v. Fayetteville State University* (1978), the university successfully dismissed a tenured professor who was charged with lack of class preparation, poor teaching, and poor relations with students. The federal district court hearing the case concluded that the university had documented adequate cause.

In addition to teaching and classroom performance, a faculty member's interactions with co-workers may also be evaluated in assessing adequate cause. Lack of mental and emotional fitness may be grounds as well for establishing adequate cause for dismissal. Incompentency, however, does not include professional judgments. A dismissed tenured faculty member had urged his students not to take northern Wisconsin teaching jobs and not to enter a graduate program where graduate students were permitted to take undergraduate courses. His dismissal was overturned in court. Further, dismissal for incompetency requires an evidentiary record that substantiates the charges.

Neglect of Duty

Neglect of duty may extend beyond teaching responsibilities to include other faculty duties as well. Faculty may be contractually required to perform duties relevant to research and teaching as well. Enforceable faculty duties include reporting requirements, committee work, maintenance of office hours, and other obligations that are shown to be job related. In such instances, failure to perform duties may be adequate grounds for dismissal if the university can document the performance failure and argue its significance persuasively (Beckham, 1986). Faculty have been fired for excessive absence or tardiness, failing to meet professional growth requirements essential for continued employment, failure to maintain office hours, and failure to appear for work at the appointed time.

In one case, a community college department chair was dismissed for failing to implement a required evaluation of his administrative performance. An Oregon appeals court hearing the case concurred that the department chair had not fulfilled his obligations. In another case, a tenured faculty member did not report, contrary to university regulation, on sponsored research grants, and after an opportunity for review by a faculty grievance committee, was dismissed. The dismissal was affirmed by a federal district court. Failing to provide adequate student supervision can also be interpreted as neglect of duties. A Wyoming music department faculty was dismissed after a hearing for allowing students to drink alcohol and smoke marijuana on a sponsored trip. The state court reviewing the case rejected the faculty member's due-process-based appeal, agreeing that the faculty member had neglected his duties to provide adequate supervision.

Insubordination

Insubordination is a willful disregard of reasonable directives from appropriate authorities or a defiant attitude of noncompliance toward regulations specifically applicable to a faculty (Beckham, 1986). In applying this ground for dismissal, the directives in question must be reasonable, rationally related to the institution's educational objectives, and unambiguous. Even so, dismissal is justified only if disobeying a directive can be shown to adversely impact on the university's pursuit of its educational goals and mission. The intent of this standard is to prevent arbitrariness and excessive discretion in using the violation of virtually any directive as the basis for dismissal.

This standard for dismissing faculty has been consistently confirmed by courts. Various university decisions to dismiss insubordinate faculty have been upheld, including the refusal of faculty to perform required duties as a protest over revision of university tenure policies and taking an unauthorized leave against the express direction of the dean. Insubordination has also been interpreted to mean persistent faculty criticisms of university administrators, amounting to "verbal attacks." Other interpretations of insubordination include employee refusal of assignments and faculty reacting in an argumentative, verbally hostile, and abusive fashion when directed to meet job requirements.

In one case, a faculty member who had been reprimanded several times for absenteeism was denied a request for a leave of absence to deliver a paper at the beginning of the semester overseas. When dismissed, he argued that his conference attendance was an expression of academic freedom. The court hearing his case sided with the university and ruled that, in light of his history of absenteeism, the university action was not excessive.

How many times may a faculty member refuse to teach a course before being dismissed, because repeated refusal to teach a required course has been interpreted as insubordination? One refusal is inadequate but may warrant a reprimand and memo stating misconduct in the employee's file. In one instance, a tenured faculty who refused to teach a course received a contract renewal saying that, if he refused to teach the course in the second year, he would be dismissed. He refused, was dismissed, and unsuccessfully sued, because the federal court concluded he had been insubordinate.

To result in dismissal that would be upheld in court, institutional requirements must be reasonable and include adequate notice. Two medical faculty who refused to comply with university requirements to sign agreements limiting their outside income were dismissed. The court agreed that the university's limits on outside income were a reasonable requirement and upheld the dismissal.

Some insubordination cases involve issues of free speech or academic freedom. A faculty member dismissed for what he claimed was his exercise of free speech sued in the case *Hillis v. Stephen F. Austin State University* (1982). The district court found for the professor. The Fifth Circuit Court of Appeals reversed a lower court and sided with the university's contention that the professor was loud, abusive, and insubordinate in his dealings with employees. Also, faculty do not have unlimited rights to say and do as they please. *Keddie v. Pennsylvania State University* (1976) identified several institutional interests limiting faculty expression. These institutional interests include ensuring discipline and harmony among coworkers, permitting confidentiality, and limiting conduct that impedes proper performance of daily duties. Other legitimate institutional interests include encouraging loyalty and confidence among employees and supervisors, allowing diversity of views and limiting classroom proselytizing, and providing orderly functioning of the university.

Immoral or Unethical Conduct

Immoral and unethical conduct by faculty has been upheld judicially as adequate cause for dismissing faculty, but court cases have not resulted in a single legal standard of what constitutes such conduct. Rather, immoral and unethical behavior has been interpreted as that which offends contemporary moral standards, is inconsistent with moral rectitude, and is generally condemned by the academic community (Beckham, 1986). In using this vague standard, the courts have employed the "detrimental" test, agreeing that universities have the right to dismiss faculty and staff whose conduct harms the educational process. The test attempts to balance these institutional needs versus the individuals' rights to live their lives as they choose. From the institutional perspective, the test emphasizes the employee's ability to perform, examining whether or not the loss of respect resulting from the allegedly immoral private action significantly impairs the faculty's ability to perform in an educational setting. Dismissal may be upheld if the employee's action results in significant loss of respect from students and colleagues and consequent unfitness to perform. In some instances, courts have allowed a brief period of time for the faculty's reputation to be restored, to preempt dismissal.

Behaviors acknowledged by the courts as immoral, unethical, and involving moral turpitude include conviction of a crime, sexual misconduct, and dishonest and ribald or vulgar behavior. Open and notorious sexual misconduct has been upheld as adequate cause, even when a direct detrimental effect on the educational process has not been proven. In some instances, the notoriety surrounding the event rather than the event itself is regarded as sufficient detriment. In one case, a faculty member and one of his students were observed parked at night in an unlit industrial area near the college partially undressed in the front seat of his car. When approached by a police officer, the faculty member became belligerent, threatened the police officer, and then tried to drive away. The court upheld the dismissal of the faculty, noting that the notoriety surrounding the case ultimately affected teaching fitness.

In one sexual harassment case, a tenured professor's dismissal was recommended by a committee established to hear charges of sexual harassment for accosting several students. When the governing board of the institution did not also hear the case but rather followed the directives of the special committee, the dismissed professor sued unsuccessfully for violation of due process. Limits on sexual harassment extend beyond students, according to a ruling by the supreme court of the state of Washington, to include sexual advances to faculty, staff, and the spouses of faculty and staff.

Additionally, sexual contact with a student not construed as harassment, particularly an undergraduate or a student in the faculty member's class, has been upheld as actionable behavior resulting in dismissal. Nor does the relationship have to be cross-gender. In one instance, a female instructor had a sexual relationship with a female undergraduate and was reassigned. Even though the instructor challenged the reassignment as bias based on sexual orientation, she lost.

Public solicitation of students is ground for dismissal. A tenured professor was arrested on a university campus for indecent acts, mostly soliciting lewd acts from students in the student union restrooms. Two different faculty hearing committees recommended only probation, but the governing board overrode the committees and dismissed the faculty member.

Criminal activity may also be interpreted as moral turpitude and, therefore, adequate cause for dismissal. In a California university, a faculty member pled guilty to grand theft for improperly billing a medical provider. Although a faculty committee did not find sufficient evidence of moral turpitude, the university president did and dismissed the faculty member. The decision of the president was supported by the California appeals court on the grounds that the faculty member's honesty had been significantly undermined.

Other cases involving moral turpitude have centered on issues of degrees and credentialing. Courts have upheld in several instances the dismissal of faculty who lied at the time they were hired about educational attainment and degrees.

Legal Bases for
Challenging Dismissals

What are the grounds you can use to challenge dismissal? What happens when you do? If you appeal the decision of your university to dismiss you to a state or federal court, the court will generally look at the legality of the process used, not its propriety (Beckham, 1986). If your university violated constitutional or statutory provisions, based decisions on unsubstantiated charges, or acted arbitrarily and capriciously with excessive discretion, the court may intervene. It will likely not intervene, however, because the court disagrees with the judgment of the university officials who made the dismissal decision. If a constitutional issue is involved, the court will adopt a strict scrutiny standard, and university administrators will be required to show compelling interests supporting their decision.

What kind of an administrative process for dismissals must universities adopt to meet court-defined adequate cause standards? Three criteria must be met. The first is that adequate cause standards must be reasonably tied to job and professional fitness. Second, any decision to dismiss must be accompanied by substantial, relevant, and credible evidence. Nor can the evidence be compromised by issues or behaviors unrelated to professional performance. Third, employment practice procedures must be clear, publicized, and properly followed.

Defendants may use several grounds to challenge dismissal, including denial of due process, free speech, association or academic freedom. Other grounds include discrimination and breach of contract (see Table 8.2).

Denial of Due Process

The Fourteenth Amendment due process clause has been interpreted to protect an employee's interest in public employment. Due process entitles an employee to take notice of

Table 8.2 Legal Bases for Challenging Dismissals

Denial of due process
> Once a prerequisite liberty or property interest is established, Fourteenth Amendment due process entitles an employee to take notice of the reasons for the university's action and an opportunity for a hearing on disputed issues of fact.

Denial of free speech, association, or academic freedom
> Protected speech must meet a four- part test, including being related to a subject of legitimate public concern.

Discrimination
> Prohibits discrimination on the basis of race, religion, national origin, sex, age, or handicap.

Breach of contract
> Occurs when institutional procedures that are part of an employment contract or have been incorporated into the terms of employment are violated and may be the primary source of legal remedy for faculty at private universities and colleges.

---

the reasons for the university's action and an opportunity for a hearing on disputed issues of fact (Beckham, 1986). In order for violation of due process to occur, the plaintiff must first establish that a liberty or property interest has been infringed. Liberty interest infringement may occur when administrative actions create or impose a stigma or other disability on the employee that impairs the faculty member's ability to gain a job elsewhere, injures the faculty member's good name, or impugns his or her good standing in the community. A property interest is infringed when the employee's "property" of entitlement to a job through negotiated agreements, contracts, and so on is affected.

Universities must meet several minimum standards to adhere to due process. Administrators must give notice of cause for termination in sufficient detail to allow the faculty to show any error that may have occurred. Dismissed faculty also are entitled to take notice of the names of witnesses and the nature of their testimony as it relates to the cause for termination. Faculty also must receive a hearing within a reasonable time in which they can respond to allegations. Finally, the hearing panel must be impartial and possess a reasonable level of expertise relative to the charges.

Denial of Free Speech, Association, or Academic Freedom

Usually, courts pay particular attention to cases that involve faculty use of free speech, a First Amendment right. In a case at San Jacinto Junior College, a woman was denied tenure in her sixth year, ostensibly for declining enrollments and poor evaluation of work, justifiable grounds. However, she was able to introduce information in court that supported her contention that true reasons for her dismissal were otherwise. She argued that she had exercised her constitutional First Amendment rights to free speech by vigorously supporting her husband's candidacy for the board of regents and supporting a faculty association. These actions, she contended, were the true cause of her dismissal. The court agreed that her constitutional rights had been violated, and a jury awarded her monetary damages.

In a series of U.S. Supreme Court cases, a legal framework was developed with a four-part test to ascertain the validity of a plaintiff's free speech claim. The employee's speech must be related to a subject of genuine public concern, therefore entitling it to constitutional protection. If the speech is protected, was the institution's response justified in terms of promoting efficiency of operations? A third test concerns whether or not the employee's protected speech was a substantial or motivating factor in the dismissal decision. And finally, if exercise of free speech were not a concern, could the employee be dismissed for adequate cause?

A major case concerning a government employee, *Connick v. Myers* (1982), was subsequently used as a precedent in higher education cases. In *Connick*, the court ruled that an employee dismissed for distributing a questionnaire about office practices had not been involved with an issue of community interest, because the questionnaire dealt primarily with her personal dispute over reassignment. Thus her dismissal was upheld. In another case, however, an avowed Marxist openly critical of textbooks and politically active for the Progressive Labor party had his job restored by the court, which ruled the behavior consistent with the exercise of free speech.

Discrimination

Both public and private universities are covered by most antidiscrimination federal and state statutes. Discrimination on the basis of race, religion, national origin, sex, age, or handicap is statutorily prohibited. The bases for these prohibitions are the equal protection clause of the Fourteenth Amendment, Title VII of the Civil Rights Act of 1964, and Title IX of the Education Amendments of 1972.

Tittle VII of the 1964 Civil Rights Act explicitly prohibits employment discrimination on the basis of race, color, religion, sex, or national origin. Employment practices that result in differential treatment of individuals or classes protected in the act are not allowed, unless employers can justify disparate treatment with a legitimate, nondiscriminatory reason, such as occupational qualification relevant to the job in question. One important case pertaining to higher education was *Board of Trustees of Keene State College v. Sweeny* (1979). Sweeny claimed sex discrimination in her denial of promotion to full professor, offering predominantly statistical evidence that women were largely confined to lower academic ranks. The college said she was not promoted due to inadequate service, particularly committee work, and personality difficulties. According to previous court rulings, the burden of proof shifted to Sweeny, who demonstrated that her previous complaints of discrimination had been ignored, and that these complaints were the source of "personality differences." She was promoted within 2 years.

Breach of Contract

Breach of contract occurs when institutional procedures that are part of an employment contract or have been incorporated into the terms of employment are violated (Beckham, 1986). Breach of contract, or contract and tort law, applies equally to public and private institutions, although other justifications for dismissal do not. Private universities and colleges are not held to the same constitutional constraints that are applied to public ones. For faculty at private institutions breach of contract may be the predominant source of legal remedy.

What defines employee contractual rights? They include verbal promises, assurances by institutional agents, institutional policy statements governing employment, and traditional custom and practice. Courts have been willing to go beyond the strict letter of the contract in resolving ambiguities. In one case in California, a court ordered an institution to restore the employment of a faculty member as long as that faculty member's grant funds were available. The courts have also interpreted usual practices surrounding the contractual relationship as part of the contract agreement.

In the ideal world, you will never be concerned with faculty dismissal procedures. Plainly, having such charges levied against you personally is very traumatic. But as Mike and Richard found out in Chapter 1, even raising questions that have the potential for leading to the dismissal of other faculty can have many repercussions. Do not go gently into this night, for gentleness is not what dismissing faculty is all about.

Conclusion

Living Happily and Ethically Ever After

This book has discussed the clash over campus ethics in universities and colleges. We have not nor could we cover all possible ethical dilemmas that you may encounter. We hope that we have, however, given you a framework to think about dilemmas you may confront and to develop strategies to deal with the dilemma. As our stories indicate, whistle-blowing when you observe wrongdoing by others is a high-cost strategy. This does not mean, however, that you should not blow the whistle. Evil persists when good people do nothing. It does mean, however, that you should carefully consider the impact whistle-blowing will have on your own career and try to shield yourself as much as possible from negative consequences. Fortunately, most people most of the time behave ethically, trying to be the best professors and administrators they can be within the institutional and cultural constraints in which they work. When you encounter the one or two potentially career-derailing episodes of unethical behavior, a wise and prudent response on your part is crucial. If you choose the high ground but think politically as well as ethically, you may be able to redress the wrongdoing while maintaining your career course. We wish you a happy and ethical future.

References

American Association of University Professors. (1989). Statement on plagiarism. *Academe, 75,* 47-48.

American Political Science Association. (1991). *A guide to professional ethics in political science.* Washington, DC: APSA Committee on Professional Ethics, Rights and Freedoms.

Beckham, J. C. (1986). *Faculty/staff nonrenewal and dismissal for cause in institutions of higher education.* Asheville, NC: College Administration Publications.

Berger, A. A. (1993). *Improving writing skills: Memos, letters, reports, and proposals.* Newbury Park, CA: Sage.

Bloom, A. (1987). *The closing of the American mind.* New York: Simon & Schuster.

Board of Trustees of Keene State College v. Sweeney, 75-182 D.N.H., April 13, 1977, appears in 14 BNA Fair Employment Prac. Cases; aff'd 569 F2d 169 (1st cir. 1978); vacated and remanded 439 U.S. 24 (1978); reaff'd 75182 D.N.H. Jan. 29, 1979, appears in 20 E.T.D. § 30278; reaff'd 604 F2d 106 (1st cir. 1979).

Bowser, B. P., Auletta, G. S., & Jones, T. (1993). *Confronting diversity issues on campus.* Newbury Park, CA: Sage.

Chung v. Park, 377 F. Supp. 524 (M. D. PA 1974), aff'd 514 F2d 382 (3rd cir. 1975).

Cole, E. K. (Ed.). (1990). *Sexual harassment on campus.* Washington, DC: National Association of College and University Attorneys.

Connick v. Myers, 507 F. Supp. 752 (E. D. LA 1981), aff'd 654 F2d 719 (5th cir. 1981), rev'd 461 U.S. 138 (1982).

Cordes, C. (1993, March 3). Research project on ear infections dramatizes challenge of conflicts. *The Chronicle of Higher Education,* pp. A23, A28.

Final findings of scientific misconduct. (1993). *NIH Guide for Grants and Contracts, 22,* 1-4.

Fox, J. A., & Levin, J. (1993). *How to work with the media.* Newbury Park, CA: Sage.

Friedman, J., Boumil, M. M., & Taylor, B. E. (1992). *Sexual Harassment.* Deerfield Beach, FL: Health Communications.

Gmelch, W. H. (1993). *Coping with faculty stress.* Newbury Park, CA: Sage.

Hillis v. Stephen F. Austin State University, 486 F. Supp. 663 (E. D. TX, Tyler Division 1980), rev'd 665 F2d 547 (5th cir. 1982).

Jawa v. Fayetteville State University, 426 f. Supp. 218 (E. D. NC 1976), aff'd 584 F2d 976 (4th cir. 1978).

Keddie v. Pennsylvania State University, 412 F. Supp. 1264 (M. D. PA 1976).

LaFollette, M. (1992). *Stealing into print: Fraud, plagiarism, and misconduct in scientific publishing.* Berkeley: University of California Press.

LaNoue, G. R., & Lee, B. A. (1987). *Academics in court.* Ann Arbor: University of Michigan.

Magner, D. K. (1993, May 12). Historian charged with plagiarism disputes critics' definition of terms. *The Chronicle of Higher Education,* pp. A16, A18-A20.

Metzger, R. O. (1993). *Developing a consulting practice.* Newbury Park, CA: Sage.

Ory, J. C., & Ryan, K. E. (1993). *Tips for improving testing and grading.* Newbury Park, CA: Sage.

Responsible science: Ensuring the integrity of the research process, Volume I. (1992). Washington, DC: National Academy Press.

Swazey, J. P., Louis, K. S., & Anderson, M. S. (1994, March 9). The ethical training of graduate students requires serious and continuing attention. *The Chronicle of Higher Education,,* pp. B1-B2.

Sykes, C. J. (1988). *Profscam: Professors and the demise of higher education.* Washington, DC: Regnery Gateway.

Weimer, M. (1993). *Improving your classroom teaching.* Newbury Park, CA: Sage.

Wheeler, D. L. (1993, May 12). Did 2 who fought research fraud for NIH go too far? *The Chronicle of Higher Education,* pp. A16, A18.

Whicker, M. L., Kronenfeld, J. J., & Strickland, R. A. (1993). *Getting tenure.* Newbury Park, CA: Sage.

Additional Readings

American Association of University Professors. (1990). *Sexual harassment: Suggested policy and procedures for handling complaints.* Washington, DC: AAUP Committee W.

American Association of University Professors. (1991a). Recommended procedural standards for dismissal proceedings in a collective bargaining setting where arbitration substitutes for a formal hearing before a body of peers. *Academe, 77,* 57.

American Association of University Professors. (1991b). Statement on intercollegiate athletics. *Academe, 77,* 49-50.

American Association of University Professors. (1991c). Statement on the "political correctness" controversy. *Academe, 77,* 48.

Barr, M. J., & Associates. (1988). *Student services and the law.* San Francisco, CA: Jossey-Bass.

Carp, R. A., & Stidham, R. (1993). *Judicial process in America* (2nd ed.). Washington, DC: CQ Press.

Carritt, E. F. (1973). *Ethical and political thinking.* Westport, CT: Greenwood.

Collis, J. (1990). *Educational malpractice.* Charlottesville, VA: Michie.

Davidson, C. N. (1991). "PH" stands for political hypocrisy." *Academe, 77,* 9-14.

DeGeorge, R. T. (Ed.). (1966). *Ethics and society.* Garden City, NY: Doubleday.

Diener, E., & Crandall, R. (1978). *Ethics in social and behavioral research.* Chicago, IL: University of Chicago Press.

Fagothey, A. (1967). *Right and reason: Ethics in theory and practice* (4th ed.). St. Louis: C. V. Mosby.

Fitzgerald, L. F. (1992). *Sexual harassment in higher education: Concepts and issues.* Washington, DC: National Education Association.

Franke, A. H., & Toll, M. A. (1989). Court decisions hinder women's, minorities' rights. *Academe, 75,* 47.

Frankena, W. K. (1973). *Ethics* (2nd ed.). Englewood Cliffs, NJ: Prentice-Hall.

Garment, S. (1991). *Scandal: The culture of mistrust in American politics.* New York: Doubleday.

Gilley, J. W., Fulmer, K. A., & Reithlingshoefer, S. J. (1986). *Searching for academic excellence.* New York: Macmillan and the American Council on Education.

Haber, J. G. (1993). *Doing and being: Selected readings in moral philosophy.* New York: Macmillan.

Kadish, M. R. (1991). *Toward an ethic of higher education.* Stanford, CA: Stanford University Press.

Kaplan, W. A. (1985). *The law of higher education* (2nd ed.). San Francisco: Jossey-Bass.

Levinson, R. M. (1989). The faculty and institutional isomorphism. *Academe, 75,* 23-27.

Lynton, E. A., & Elman, S. E. (1987). *New priorities for the university.* San Francisco: Jossey-Bass.

May, W. W. (Ed.). (1990). *Ethics and higher education.* New York: Macmillan and the American Council on Education.

Menand, L. (1993). The future of academic freedom. *Academe, 79,* 11-17.

Metzger, W. P. (1977). *The constitutional status of academic tenure.* New York: Arno.

Owens, H. F. (Ed.). (1984). *Risk management and the student affairs professional* (Vol. 2., NASPA Monograph Series). Washington, DC: National Association of Student Personnel Administrators.

Stern, C. S. (1993, March 10). Colleges must be careful not to write bad policies on sexual harassment. *The Chronicle of Higher Education*, pp. B1, B2.

Ulbrich, H. H. (1989). Departmental takeover and the peculiar property rights of academics. *Academe, 75*, 33-35.

Wagner, E. N. (1993, May 26). Fantasies of true love in academe. *Chronicle of Higher Education*, pp. B1-B3.

Wilshire, B. (1990). *The moral collapse of the university.* Albany: State University of New York Press.

Young, D. P., & Gehring, D. D. (1986). *The college student and the courts* (rev. ed.). Asheville, NC: College Administration Publications.

About the Authors

Marcia Lynn Whicker (Ph.D., University of Kentucky, 1976) is Professor of Public Administration at the Graduate School at Rutgers, Newark. Her publications include 12 books, more than 45 peer-reviewed articles, and more than 50 nonpeer-reviewed and journalistic articles in the areas of public policy, public administration, and United States politics. Her interests include using computer-simulation models to test the effectiveness and representativeness of governmental structures and systems.

Jennie Jacobs Kronenfeld (Ph.D., Brown University, 1976) is Professor of Health Administration in the College of Business at Arizona State University in Tempe. She has published 5 books and 100 articles in the areas of health services research, health administration, health education, health policy, and women and health. She also has specialized in survey research on health issues.